Architectural Design

Islam + Architecture
Guest-edited by Sabiha Foster

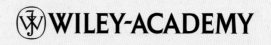 WILEY-ACADEMY

Architectural Design
Vol 74 No 6 (Nov/Dec 2004)

ISBN 0470090944
Profile No 172

Editorial Offices
International House
Ealing Broadway Centre
London W5 5DB
T: +44 (0)20 8326 3800
F: +44 (0)20 8326 3801
E: architecturaldesign@wiley.co.uk

Editor
Helen Castle

Production
Mariangela Palazzi-Williams

Art Direction/Design
Christian Küsters (CHK Design)

Design Assistant
Hannah Dumphy (CHK Design)

**Project Coordinator
and Picture Editor**
Caroline Ellerby

Advertisement Sales
01243 843272

Abbreviated positions:
b=bottom, c=centre, l=left, r=right

Cover design by Sabiha Foster

AD
pp 5-12 © Mandy Bates; pp 13-17 courtesy Mandy Bates; pp 18, 20 & 21(t) © Nasser Rabbat; p 21(b) © Aga Khan Award for Architecture, photo courtesy of the architect; p 22 courtesy Walter Denny; p 23 © Aga Khan Award for Architecture, photo Reha Günay; pp 24 & 25(b) © Aga Khan Award for Architecture, photos Mohammed Akram; p 25(t) © Aga Khan Award for Architecture, photo Reha Günay; p 26 © Aga Khan Award for Architecture, photo Hassaan Gardezi; p 27 © Aga Khan Award for Architecture, photo Christopher Little; pp 28 & 31 © Aga Khan Award for Architecture, photos Ram Rahman; p 29 © Aga Khan Award for Architecture, photo Christian Richters; p 30 © Aga Khan Award for Architecture, photo courtesy of the architect; pp 32-6 © Aga Khan Award for Architecture/Barefoot Architects of Tilonia; pp 38-43 courtesy William R Polk; pp 46 & 53(b) © F Sahba, photos Raghu Rai; p 47 courtesy F Sahba; pp 48-51 © F Sahba, photos Omid Yazdani; pp 52 & 53(t) © Mandy Bates; p 55 © Center for the Study of the Built Environment (CSBE), drawings by Hind Hussein; p 56 © Aga Khan Award for Architecture, photo Christopher Little; p 57 © Aga Khan Award for Architecture, photo KL Ng; p 58(t) © Aga Khan Award for Architecture, photo Samir Saddi; p 58(b) © Center for the Study of the Built Environment (CSBE), photo Mohammad al-Asad; pp 60 & 62 courtesy of the Aga Khan Award for Architecture; p 61 © Aga Khan Award for Architecture, photo Pascal Maréchaux; pp 64-8 © Turgut Cansever; pp 71-7 courtesy Keith Critchlow; pp 78-83 © Mohamed El-Husseiny; pp 84-9 © Hashim Sarkis Architecture and Urban Design; p 90 © Shinkenchiku-sha; pp 91(t) & 93 © Aga Khan Award for Architecture; p 91(b) © Cengiz Bektas; p 92(l) © Doğan Tekeli, photo Cemal Endem; p 92(tr) © Behruz Çinici; p 92(br) © Tuncay Çavdar; p 94 © GAD Architecture, photo Esma Sultan; p 96 © Semra Uygur/Özcan Uygur; pp 98 & 102 © AMO/OMA (Office for Metropolitan Architecture); p 99 © Esra Akcan; p 100 courtesy Esra Akcan; p 101 Reprinted with permission of Simon & Schuster Adult Publishing Group, from *The Clash of Civilizations and the Remaking of World Order* by Samuel P Huntington © 1996 Samuel P Huntington, base map © Hammond World Atlas Corp; pp 105-9 courtesy of Zaha Hadid Architects.

2+
pp 112-17 © Sinan Hassan; pp 118-19 © Stephen R Thomas/Renaissance Services; p 120(tr) © 2x4; p 120(br) © 2x4, photo Mark Schendel; p 120(cb) courtesy of Prada; p 120(tl&bl) & 121 © Sharon Dang/Pixel Clinic; pp 122-3 & 124(t) © Ruedi Walti; p 124(b) & 125 © Herzog & De Meuron; pp 126-7 © Farrow Partnership Architects, Inc, photos Peter Sellar/Klik Photography.

Subscription Offices UK
John Wiley & Sons Ltd.
Journals Administration Department
1 Oldlands Way, Bognor Regis
West Sussex, PO22 9SA
T: +44 (0)1243 843272
F: +44 (0)1243 843232
E: cs-journals@wiley.co.uk

Annual Subscription Rates 2004
Institutional Rate: UK £175
Personal Rate: UK £99
Student Rate: UK £70
Institutional Rate: US $270
Personal Rate: US $155
Student Rate: US $110
AD is published bi-monthly.
Prices are for six issues and include postage and handling charges. Periodicals postage paid at Jamaica, NY 11431. Air freight and mailing in the USA by Publications Expediting Services Inc, 200 Meacham Avenue, Elmont, NY 11003

Single Issues UK: £22.50
Single Issues outside UK: US $45.00
Details of postage and packing charges available on request

Postmaster
Send address changes to AD Publications Expediting Services, 200 Meacham Avenue, Elmont, NY 11003

Printed in Italy. All prices are subject to change without notice. [ISSN: 0003-8504]

Islam + Architecture
Guest-edited by Sabiha Foster

The international field of architecture has become a world dominated by blobs, curves and self-referential verbiage. This was most conspicuously displayed this autumn at the opening of the 2004 Architecture Biennale in Venice. The exhibited schemes are with few exceptions ingenious and formally impressive, with an accompanying narrative that is often highfalutin jargon and, at times, nonsensical. The biennale is at a generative design and engineering level an exceptional show; one cannot fail to be heartened by the fact that such high-quality, experimental architecture is being commissioned and constructed, perhaps more widely than ever before. However, it cannot be ignored that most of the projects originate from the US and the wealthier nations of Europe. (One of the few Middle Eastern schemes, the Alexandria Library, is by the Norwegian firm Snøhetta.) Overall, the selection gives the impression that the Middle East, much of Asia, most of Africa and even Australia are being sidelined. This is certainly not intentional; Belgium's national pavilion was laudably awarded with the show's prize for breaking the mould and exploring the urban form of a city in the Congo. Nevertheless, the geographic lines of the exhibition are, given present economic and cultural forces, almost inevitable – though not wholly: Australia, which has been the site of some very strong schemes in this ilk, seemed to all intents and purposes to have disappeared! (The curating of this year's exhibition certainly expressed a strong North American bias.)

While it is important that acknowledgement and recognition is given to high-quality architectural design, it is also essential that the world of architecture does not become circumvented and centred on a few privileged Western institutions – in terms of design pedagogy and graduate output. If life is an inexorable undertaking of delicate counterbalances, then we are at a crucial point in time when architecture needs to look up and beyond its own internal preoccupations and form-finding. Architects, architectural educators, editors and writers cannot afford to become blinkered and lose sight of the wider world. This autumn we passed the third anniversary of 9/11, and a fair number of dedicated TV documentaries and generous column inches were devoted to speculation of the advancement of the development of Ground Zero – a quite small, if very significant, site in Manhattan. In terms of media coverage, at least, it seems the fascination with Daniel Libeskind's ability to assert his position as a master planner far outweighs the more fundamental job in hand for the international community of ensuring the reconstruction of war-torn Iraq and Afghanistan.

In the 1980s there was, at least, a flurry of interest around Hassan Fathy and the schemes encouraged by the admirable work of the Aga Khan foundation. This was reflected in the pages of *Architectural Design* and some dedicated monographs produced by Academy Editions. One of the few pluses of Postmodernism was that it encouraged a cultural eclecticism, which may have been magpie-like in its acquisition of other cultural and historical styles, but was at the same time ostensibly outward-looking. It also encouraged scholarship and investment in publications for the consumption of architects beyond the immediate contemporary net.

This title of *Architectural Design* is a very important call for understanding. It asks architects and those engaged in architectural culture to look beyond what is currently put in front of them. By devoting an entire issue to Islam and its relationship with architecture, the quest has been to reveal and discuss the divergence of Islamic culture across the globe. The approach has been one of opening up what is currently understood by 'the Islamic', rather than narrowing down to a definition that would allow one to create an accessible digest of the subject for easy consumption. The theme of pluralism is eloquently introduced by the guest-editor, Sabiha Foster, through her thought-provoking text on multiplicity in unity; diversity is further explored at a historical level by Professor Nasser Rabbat, as he exposes ancient lines of cross-cultural exchange, and underlined by Suha Özkan, whose article highlights the very breadth of architectural treatments in Islamic lands. This is further shored up by giving over space to architecture in particular geographical contexts (Egypt, the Lebanon and Turkey), a focus which is taken to practice level in Sabiha Foster's profile of Sinan Hassan, a US-educated architect who has returned to work in Syria. Jeremy Melvin's article on Islam and the avant-garde throws up links between some of the strongest exponents of current experimental architecture – Zaha Hadid, Farshid Moussavi of FOA, and Hani Rashid of Asymptote – who, with their Middle Eastern backgrounds, display an innate empathy and understanding of complex geometries: a reassertion, perhaps, of the need to reconnect and discover what appears to lie beyond us in order to enrich what lies directly in front of us. △

Multiplicity in Unity

Architecture addresses our metaphysical, philosophical and cultural identities within a material context. It challenges us to look at history and, therefore, at architecture in a new way. An evaluation of architecture must essentially be an evaluation of ourselves. And an evaluation of ourselves demands that we situate ourselves within the evolving meanings of our histories and traditions.

'Everything is:
The shadows in the glass
Which, in between the day's two twilights, you
Have scattered by the thousands,
Or shall strew henceforward in the mirrors
that you pass.
And everything is part of that diverse
Crystalline memory, the universe.'[1]

The principle of unity is fundamental to Islamic art and architecture. Although the square and the rectangle have harmonious proportions, the circle is the ultimate expression of unity. The circle contains polygons, both containing and underlying it. It produces triangles, squares and hexagons. In Islamic symbology, devolved from Egyptian, Indian and Greek geometry, the square is equated with the earth, or materiality, the triangle with human consciousness, and the hexagon or circle with creation.

Top
All Islamic patterns begin with the circle and its centre. In order to create repetitive patterns, Islamic designers repeated the circle. The circle encloses every conceivable symmetry. If identical copies of a circle are placed together with their outermost edges touching, so that they retain their separate identity while also becoming part of a larger shape, their centres rather than their edges become the point at which lines are connected. If we join the centres of three united circles, we create an equilateral triangle.

Bottom
An equilateral triangle within the larger triangle. To demonstrate the complexity of symmetry we can draw three circles with half the radius of the original circles around the points at which the original circles touch the others, and produce an exact replication of the original figure. This repetition can repeat infinitely, and is how patterns in Islamic art and architecture were created.

'Multiplicity in unity' as a transforming power is of great significance. It is the central tenet of Islam[2] that inspired the writings of Islamic philosophers such as the 12th-century Sufi, Ibn 'Arabi,[3] and, redefined as pluralism, it is the philosopher Isaiah Berlin's[4] most compelling idea. Berlin, one of the 20th-century's most significant historians of ideas, said that all values are plural, and that there is no single solution to the moral questions facing humanity. To believe that there is, is to mistake the essence of human values. By 'plural' it is meant that all values are genuine, and thus cannot possibly be interpreted, redefined or incorporated in a mother of all values.

This perspective suggests that it simply isn't possible to create a blueprint for human life, because genuine values are almost always incompatible and incommensurable, something which is best illustrated by many of the issues we are concerned with today: more equality, less liberty; more efficiency, less spontaneity; more development, less sustainability; more market rights, less human rights. And this is why it is difficult to find resolution in conflict situations; there is no single 'referee' value to help us balance one value against another.

Values create the ways of life that we describe as cultures. Pluralism is relevant to architecture in that the value systems of diverse cultural traditions are completely separate values. Our common understanding of tradition, as

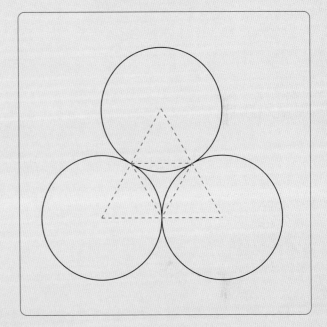

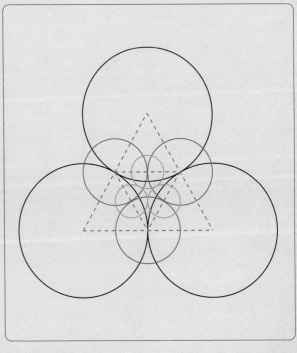

Architecture cannot be disassociated from its ideological and political context, thus we need to look at what notions of identity, culture, tradition and history represent. To understand the past we must develop a feeling for how it relates to the present. 'Tradition is a matter of much wider significance. It cannot be inherited, and if you want it you must obtain it by great labour,' wrote TS Eliot.

something 'pure', mysteriously rooted in our pasts and transmitted to us in hermetically sealed form, is far removed from reality. Although historians tell us that traditions can be successfully invented, as was the case in imperial Britain,[5] by and large traditions evolve naturally. So however much we may cling to the singularity and uniqueness of a tradition, at its core a tradition is nothing more than the evolution of a 'single', volatile, multistrand culture that is passed on to successive generations.

Architecture cannot be disassociated from its ideological and political context, thus we need to look at what notions of identity, culture, tradition and history represent. To understand the past we must develop a feeling for how it relates to the present. 'Tradition is a matter of much wider significance. It cannot be inherited, and if you want it you must obtain it by great labour,' wrote TS Eliot.[6] Both Christianity and Islam are rooted in the Judaic tradition, and whatever it is we classify as Western civilisation developed long before Greece or Rome. Civilisations flourished in Mesopotamia, Egypt and, further afield, India and China. First-century BC Alexandria, on the coast of Egypt, was the centre of Mediterranean learning, and it was here that Greek science and philosophy met with ancient Egyptian and Eastern scholarship, out of which encounter Hermeticism and Neoplatonism were born.

Greek heritage was a rich bouillon of Mediterranean concepts, put into a dialectical recipe by the Greeks. Similarly, the Roman Empire thrived because of its ability to assimilate the cultures and traditions of the peoples it conquered. When, in the 7th century, Islam became heir to what had been, it began to fuse the long-forgotten constituent elements of Hellenistic science into a powerful, unifying concept. It then went on to make original and inventive contributions of its own in the vital areas of mathematics, algebra, algorithms, science, astronomy, law, history, medicine, pharmacology, optics, agriculture, art, architecture, theology, music and poetry.

Through its assimilation of the cultures and traditions of the various peoples it conquered, Islam succeeded in unifying the sacred and the secular. Its sense of community evolved from a pluralism that celebrated difference as diversity, and diversity as unity, an approach that created an ethic of community that transcended political boundaries. All true religions inspire models for society that transcend personal ambition and ego. However, this does not mean that ignorance, radical interpretations and zealotry cease to exist. Early Islamic societies were no different. The fanaticism of orthodoxy destroyed great Sufi teachers such as al-Hallaj[7] and Suhrawardi Maqtul.[8] But despite such abhorrent excesses, by and large moderation and enlightenment prevailed because the core teachings[9] of Islam, based on the doctrine of unity, proved to be more powerful than any intolerant, self-righteous leaders.

In 1582, a time when Britain was burning heretics at the stake, the emperor Akbar was proclaiming the importance of religious freedom and formulating a code of religious behaviour amidst weekly discussions that included not only secular Muslim scholars but also Hindu, Jain, Christian, Jewish and Zoroastrian theologians. The mystical dimension of Islam's central tenet was manifested in a tolerance that was exceptional for its time; this is why Islamic societies became cosmopolitan melting pots, pluralistic societies which recognised and worked with the potential of diverse populations, including Christian, Jewish and other traditions.

But empires rise and fall. Islam's 800 years of power, which had spanned half the globe, came to an end between the 18th and 19th centuries when the Middle East was colonised by European powers and the Islamic Central Asian states absorbed by Soviet Russia. True, there are no empires today, but history does not have the tidiness of fiction, and it may well be that the processes that produced the empires of the past have morphed into more subtle ones with not dissimilar objectives. The feeling that the Great Game is still being played, albeit by more lateral means, seems to be at the source of some of the unrest of the 21st century. Indeed, these lateral means may even have led to some of the problems we face today.

Much has been written about the Islamic peoples' supposed resistance to modernisation. But such a view is a facile dismissal of deeper issues that are to do with political circumstances – issues beyond social control. In the last century, peoples' sense of identity was undermined by Orientalist[10] policies. It is now being undermined by feelings of powerlessness in the face of seemingly unmanageable political and economic odds.

> The main reason for so-called Islamic 'resistance to all things modern' lies not in a rejection of modernity or modernisation, but in an awareness of what is happening to the West where local, cultural and regional identities are being erased by an all-pervading market culture.

The main reason for so-called Islamic 'resistance to all things modern' lies not in a rejection of modernity or modernisation, but in an awareness of what is happening to the West where local, cultural and regional identities are being erased by an all-pervading market culture. There is awareness in Islamic societies that the encroaching global market culture has fragmented the 'modernised' West's perception of what identity, culture, tradition and values actually mean. Thus there is a genuine anxiety that the juggernaut of commercial interests smothers the rich variety of differences that make people human. This wariness creates confusion about 'identity' and values, which makes people vulnerable to exploitation by radical forces who rally the dispossessed and the unacknowledged under damaging and falsely unifying slogans.

We know that no religion was ever created as the basis for the legal foundation of nation-states; we know that there is no evidence to suggest that any religion was ever conceived of as anything other than a way of personal conduct. However, just as in the past the Christian church initiated eight centuries of the Inquisition,[11] and Nazi excesses were generated in a 'Christian' country, we now see 'neo-conservative' fundamentalist Christianity gaining ground in the US, and in India radical Hinduism wreaking havoc on minority populations. Today's great tragedy is that Islam, once the religion of unity and tolerance, is being undermined by radical interpretations that stand in direct opposition to the enlightened interpretations that once inspired and unified Islamic societies.

In a recent article in the *Guardian* newspaper, William Dalyrymple wrote: 'Ever since the 1930s, the Saudis have promoted Wahhabism, the most severe incarnation of Islam. After the oil boom of the early 1970s this became a fundamental tenet of Saudi foreign policy, and a sizeable slice of the country's vast oil revenues has been devoted to promoting Wahhabism at the expense of more tolerant forms of Islam. The Saudis have provoked a clash of civilisations, not so much between East and West as within Islam itself. The Wahhabis have always been opponents of Sufism: on coming to power in the early 19th century, the Wahhabis destroyed all the Sufi and Shia shrines in Arabia and Iraq. At the time, most Muslims regarded the Wahhabis as an extreme and alien sect. But in recent years the Wahhabis have used their oil revenues to attempt to remake Islam in their own puritanical image.'[12]

Mr Dalyrymple goes on to say that: 'The Saudis now dominate as much as 95 per cent of Arabic language media; 80 per cent of mosques in the US are controlled by Wahhabi imams. While limiting radical Islam at home, the Saudis have promoted it abroad, principally by funding hardcore Wahhabi and Salafi schools in the Muslim world, most concertedly in Afghanistan, Kurdistan and Pakistan.'

Damaging, exclusive and radical versions of Islam that are not accepted by the majority of Muslims have the power to affect the dispossessed and the alienated, and to create a distortion in people's sense of themselves and their consequent dogmatic rejection of others. The worry is that alienation from enlightened mainstream Islam may become so profound that the alienated minority may see itself only as members of the ulema[13] and not simultaneously as members of a pluralist, multifaith, multicultural global community that needs to unite in order to face the challenges that confront us all.

Continuity, in its historical and archetypal sense, resides only in our collective human experience. A history is never a single story but rather an extended network of histories. Edward Said said that the reality for much of history has always been a collection of cultures and civilisations, which were interdependent, flowing into and out of each other. Our modern nation-states, based on exclusive ethnic and religious identity, suppress that reality. Of our unresolved sense of identity, Said says: 'The terrible conflicts that herd people under falsely unifying rubrics such as "America", "the West" or "Islam" and invent collective identities for large numbers of individuals who are actually quite diverse, cannot remain as potent as they are, and must be opposed.'[14] Linda Colley, one of today's most significant historians, studies issues of the past that inform the present, and maintains that history can best be experienced as a guide to the future, though only if we resist the temptation to clothe it in self-satisfying myths of our own devising.[15] We know that there is no 'pure' religion,[16] and contemporary historical research and science are now revealing that there is no 'pure' race, nor any societies, cultures or traditions that can claim to be 'pure'. By definition, human beings and human cultures are hybrids.[17]

By today's nationalist reckonings, St Augustine, the founder of the Christian church, was an Algerian born in a place now called Souk-Ahras, and St George, the patron saint of England, a Turk. Numerous Roman emperors[18] came from Rome's conquered provinces. Despite English claims to its singular culture, historians, linguists and Melvyn Bragg tell us that England is a hybrid nation with a hybrid culture and a hybrid language, and that our green and pleasant land's splendid multiform richness comes from its mongrel status: over a hundred other languages give us 'English' words such as: eggs, paradigm, shampoo, azimuth, arsenal, algorithm, admiral, algebra, alcove, turquoise, tycoon, canyon, pariah, aniline, paradise, vigilante, gingham, loiter, prestige, balderdash, bloom, nudge and poppycock. Similarly, architecture, whether Romanesque, Gothic, Palladian or Saracenic, is inspired by imported forms, and 'English' gardens contain hundreds of 'classic English' plants brought here from foreign lands. Our new-found concepts of nations and of nation-states obscure perception of the dazzling multiplicity that creates the oneness of humanity. Today, more vividly than ever, our nation-states are a multiplicity of diasporic identities that have the potential to help us perceive identity as sameness rather than difference.

To understand Islam's architecture we have to go beyond he jargon of elevations and openings, and develop an understanding of its inner rationale. Islamic architecture was always of its time; modern, hi-tech, revolutionary and forward looking. Centuries before computer-instigated geometry, through its knowledge of abstract mathematical symbols and their unifying relation to the various orders of reality, Islam aimed to relate the material world to its basic abstract principle. One can't get more hi-tech than that.

Ancient Mesopotamian,[19] Egyptian[20] and Indian civilisations, and other spiritual traditions,[21] including

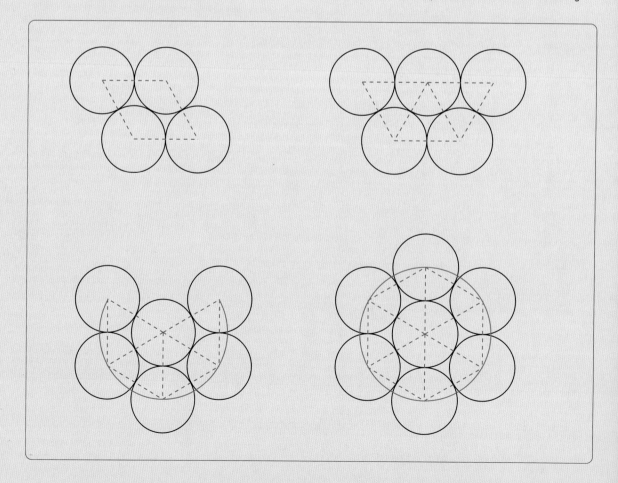

Right
Adding more circles
creates larger polygons.

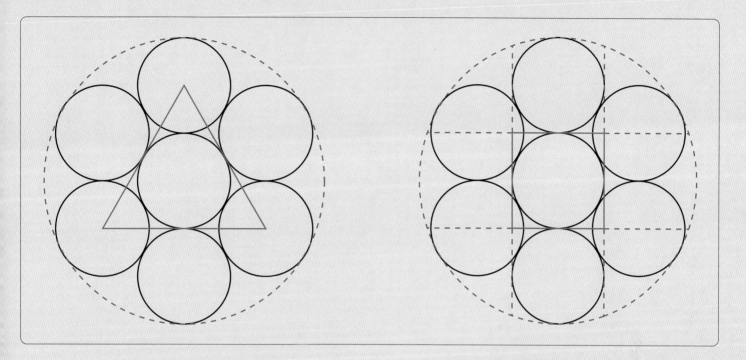

the Jewish Qabala, Gnostic Christianity and mystical Islam, all claimed that the very structure of Creation lies within geometry and numbers.[22] It was believed that architecture in its highest form was the external expression of an inner spatial sense, an inherent knowing inspired in the right 'mode' in the knower. From Edirne to Hyderabad, from Fez to Isfahan, from the domes of Shia mosques to the *muqarnas*[23] at the Alhambra palace, and from Baghdad's 7th-century city plan to rural courtyard houses, Islamic architecture expressed the *batin*, the inner abstract aspect of Islam. This abstract discipline inspired buildings that were socially responsible, ecologically sound and harmoniously avant-garde.

Islam's inventiveness in the use of geometry also had a profound effect on architecture in Europe.[24] It is interesting to consider that without Islam's architectural innovations, many of the late-Renaissance campaniles in Italy may never have been built, and there might also never have been a St Paul's Cathedral in London,[25] since Christopher Wren's masterpiece has its origins in his fascination with Islamic forms. Indeed, as any close comparative analysis reveals, without the transmission of Islamic knowledge to Europe there may not have been a Renaissance or an Enlightenment to speak of.

Globalisation, and the games it generates, need a revision of the rules, but there is no sign of this happening quite yet. This means that our pursuit of the pluralist approach is all the more relevant if conditions in the Middle East and

elsewhere remain unstable for years to come. It can be said that democracy 'took in' Europe because poverty, inequality and injustice, and their potential to run amok, were held at bay with the sop of state education, health, housing and unemployment benefits. Without similar welfare-state buffering, democracy may not 'take in' the Islamic Middle East, yet there is no public discussion of this at the present time. 'Freedom without opportunity', as Noam Chomsky says, 'is the devil's gift'.[26] The other difficulty is that elections are not necessarily synonymous with democracy. In Indonesia, Pakistan and the Middle East, for example, we see local elites who hold on to power by indirectly electing an upper house who can veto legislation. The main obstacle to economic reform in Islamic areas has not been a lack of expertise, but a lack of will on the part of local regimes to implement reform. But in time there will be more to contend with: the 'tyranny of the majority' de Tocqueville speaks of suggests that even democracies can be authoritarian or liberal, as the effect of neo-conservative thinking on democracy can create material satisfaction and indifference to the beliefs that nurture consideration for the rights of others.

The essence of life, politics, architecture and everything is the balancing of priorities, and this requires a pluralistic perspective, as both Ibn 'Arabi and Isaiah Berlin would agree.

We cannot truly comprehend the overwhelmingly complex unity of our globalised world, for the dominant forms of cultural, economic and political life are more enmeshed today than ever before. But it should matter to us that we walk towards a world that cultivates a sense of the whole, along with an awareness of how things relate to one another. The *safiye batin*, the inner

Our objective in terms of architecture is perhaps one of locating a social conscience within the incompatible values of globalisation and identity, between the heroic concept of sustainable development and survival itself. We cannot create a blueprint for architecture or for life, but we can live better in our times if we have defined the terms of our existence: in defining the terms we can hope to influence and transform the rules of the game. Thus the Islamic world is the ideal space for discussion and practice of the cultural and social issues of architecture.

teachings of Islam, say that true communication can come only from the heart. Such awareness demands that we seek a new kind of universalism, in theory and in practice, which acknowledges, respects and celebrates human diversity.

Steel, glass and concrete have long been associated with forward–looking attitudes, but modernity is not a style with standardised rules any more than 'Islamic architecture' is a style that requires appliqués of regional pastiche or the extravagance of random arches and plonk-on, precast domes. Mnemosyn, the Greek goddess of memory and the muses, does not differentiate between the past and the future. She holds us in the past as she projects us towards the future. The Urdu and Hindi word for yesterday and tomorrow is the same – *kal*. We can, from our place in the present, recognise the past and respect it for what it has to offer the present. But how do we, as architects and designers, create a culturally and environmentally valid architecture that is sensitive to a multiplicity of traditions without allowing subjective values and images to intervene in the design process?

We need an openness of spirit to see that the setting up, as an absolute priority, of any

one thing – of hi-tech architectural applications or traditional constructions, democratic capitalism or economic integration, or anything else to the exclusion of other supporting values – is unintelligent. We have to recognise that we cannot drill or conquer our way out of problems. In a world of accelerated change, unstable conditions and limited resources, we need to adapt our ways of thinking and look unflinchingly at the realm of ideas. Architecture today is a brilliantly packaged and masterfully marketed commodity – it's thrilling, exciting and fun – but by and large the model remains a passive one; it keeps its distance, its air of knowing better. Can we begin to involve ourselves with the values architecture reflects, inspires and should speak for? Can architecture accept responsibility for social and political concerns, and do so within the realities that confront us? Can we leave the subject open to the poetics of imagination which architecture depends on for its vitality?

Our objective in terms of architecture is perhaps one of locating a social conscience within the incompatible values of globalisation and identity, between the heroic concept of sustainable development and survival itself. We cannot create a blueprint for architecture or for life, but we can live better in our times if we have defined the terms of our existence: in defining the terms we can hope to influence and transform the rules of the game. Thus the Islamic world is the ideal space for discussion and practice of the cultural and social issues of architecture.

The Aga Khan has often suggested that the reawakening of inheritance and the nurturing of its continuing evolution can demonstrate how cultural pluralism can enable the Islamic world to provide innovative solutions to a wide range of contemporary

problems, such as ethnic and religious conflict, the growth of slums, the devaluation of distinctive traditions, social exclusion and the dehumanisation of the built environment. As the work of the Aga Khan Award for Architecture reveals,[27] there are Islamic communities[28] involved in dealing effectively with sensitive issues such as land tenure, cultural identity and historical consciousness. There is evidence of innovative low-cost engineering and enlightened land ordinances, of the 'daring confrontation between tradition, landscape, and high technology',[29] sensitively designed responses to the special needs of society,[30] cultural complexes[31] that incorporate innovative use of indigenous materials and traditional forms, and art and architectural traditions that are integrated in humanised modern[32] buildings.

As our world erupts in a violent clamour for recognition and justice, we find ourselves defined by our fragmented external circumstances, whereas our true identity waits to be inspired from within ourselves. This may be why the transforming power of pluralism eludes us. It is perhaps time that we look at the inner heart of our religions with the highest aspect of our intellects, and accept that reform can begin only with our own mindful consciousness of our perception of multiplicity as unity as the relationship between everything and Everything.

The challenge for us today is to face the dominant themes of our time. Civilisation cannot be founded on fashion shows, art galleries and opera houses; it must have its roots in our feeling for freedom, justice and human dignity for all. These values are dear to every human heart, and it is only the hubris and hypocrisy of politics that pretends otherwise.

How can architecture engage with our plural values? Is there a concept that transcends our ideas of territorial space? Can we recognise the specific and the transcendent, the counterpoint and the overtone, in a manner that is not adversarial but accepts the crises that confront us? If we succeed in grounding ourselves in this awareness we can work from within the opportunities and conditions of today's world to create a future that can hold its head in the heavens of idealism and remember, as St Bernard de Clairvaux said, that: 'God is length, width, height and depth.'

The visionary Buckminster Fuller questioned whether a structure existed that was common to both physical and metaphysical reality, and attempted to understand life by the abstractions of geometry and numbers. Like early medieval Islamic philosophers, Fuller could not separate the idea of technology from the natural world, and his lifelong goal was to anticipate solving humanity's major problems through the highest technology by providing 'more and more life support for everybody, with less and less resources'. Such an approach, true to the spirit of pluralism, suggests that we look more closely at the development of new combinations of metals and elements, and create materials with varying structural characteristics and functional propensities. The high tensile qualities inherent in these materials could be used most effectively by taking an entirely new approach to design itself.

> It doesn't have to be either/or. We cannot hyphenate humanity. It is possible to learn from the creative processes of the past while resisting the urge to replicate and imitate past architectural forms.

What shall we do – remain tied to the past or tie ourselves blindly to the present? It doesn't have to be either/or. We cannot hyphenate humanity. It is possible to learn from the creative processes of the past while resisting the urge to replicate and imitate past architectural forms.

Unity is plural and at minimum two. According to Ibn 'Arabi, one eye need not be sacrificed for the other. We learn to integrate and unify only when we learn to see with both eyes: the eye of reason and the eye of insight. The Aga Khan[33] has warned that: 'Loss of this inheritance of pluralism and the identity it conveys to members of diverse societies, and the originality it represents and stimulates in all of them will impoverish our societies now and into the future.' At a time when the debate has so much to do with culture, tradition, identity and values, we need to find new ways of thinking. The Aga Khan reflects the essence of Islamic teachings when he emphasises the embodiment of values: 'There are many interpretations of Islam within the wider Islamic community, but generally we are instructed to leave the world a better place than it was when we came into it. The value system of Islam, in terms of the relationship between what we call *din* and *dunia*, that is, the world and faith, is very particular in Islam. In a sense they relate to each other in an ongoing way.'[34]

As for the relevance of Islam, Prince Charles puts it simply: 'Islam is part of our past and present, in all fields of human endeavour. It has helped to create modern Europe. It is part of our own inheritance, not a thing apart.'

Notes

1 Jorge Luis Borges, in Alexander Coleman (ed), *Selected Poems*, Viking, 1999.

2 The *tauhid*.

3 Ibn 'Arabi, AD 1165–1240. The idea, implicit throughout Ibn 'Arabi's writings, is *wahdat al-wojud* – 'the oneness of being'. 'Arabi rejected the authorities who said that *tashbih* (God manifest in creation) was a heresy. He said that *tashbih* was the necessary complement of *tanzih* (declaring God incomparable with creation). This perspective led to a harmonisation of reason and 'unveiling'; that is, insight, imagination and divinely inspired intuition. 'Arabi's influence is on the increase, both in the Islamic world and in the West. (See www.ibnarabisociety.org)

4 Isaiah Berlin, philosopher, political theorist, essayist. Works by Berlin include: *Liberty* (2002); *Three Critics of the Enlightenment* (2000); and *The Crooked Timber of Humanity: Chapters in the History of Ideas* (1990).

5 Eric Hobsbawm and Terence Ranger (eds), *The Invention of Tradition*, Cambridge University Press, 1992. Contributors: Hugh Trevor Roper, Prys Morgan, David Cannadine and Bernard S Cohen, Terence Ranger. Historical research reveals that many British traditions presented as ancient are recent inventions.

6 TS Eliot, *The Sacred Wood: Essays on Poetry and Criticism*, Methuen (London), 1920.

7 One of the most influential early Sufis, Mansur al-Hallaj, was executed in AD 922.

8 Suhrawardi Maqtul, although nominally not a Sufi, is the founder of the 12th-century *Ishraqi*, or Illuminationist School of Islamic philosophy.

9 Islam believes that the revelation granted to the prophet Mohammed is the continuation of the 'pure' distilled faith of Adam and Abraham, and it is therefore the restoration of a preordained, primordial and fundamental unity that began with Abraham and passed to Jesus Christ.

10 Edward Said argued that Orientalism, although it claimed to be a disinterested field, in fact functioned to serve political ends: Western writers and academics have misrepresented, and still misrepresent, the Islamic world in a manner that has eased the way for the West to dominate the East. Orientalism thus became part of the imperial conceit and provided the rationale for Western imperialism, which could be described as the redemption of a degenerate world. Said was a polymath, literary critic, writer, professor at Columbia, a man of intellect and integrity, and a critic not only of US and Israeli policy, but also equally of the Palestinian leadership and of Arab governments in general. 'It is the role of the Arab intellectual,' he wrote, 'to articulate and defend the principles of liberation and democracy at all costs.' His many books include *Freud and the Non-European* (2003). In *Moses and Monotheism*, Freud proposes that Moses was Egyptian: in *Freud and the Non-European*, Said explores Freud's assumption for Middle Eastern politics, and says that Israel's march towards an exclusively Jewish state denies any sense of a complex, inclusive past, suggesting that an unresolved, nuanced sense of identity might, if embodied in political reality, form the basis for a new understanding between Jews and Palestinians.

11 Pope Innocent III instituted the Inquisition, a punishment for heresy, in the 12th century, and it lasted well into the late 18th century. Punishments ranged from extreme physical abuse and torture to burning at the stake. Initially, the Inquisition dealt only with Christian heretics, but later the church objected to the great Jewish sage and philosopher Maimonides' writings (a synthesis of Judaism and other cultures), providing it with a pretext for mass burnings of Jews. The Inquisition spread to Spanish and Portuguese colonies in the New World and Asia; branches operated in Goa, Brazil, Mexico, the Philippines, Guatemala, Peru, New Granada and the Canary Islands.

12 *Guardian*, 14 June 2004.

13 The international community of Muslims.

14 From Said's last book, *Freud and the Non-European*, Verso (London), 2003.

15 Colley writes of the historical development of a sense of British national identity, nationhood and nationalism. She has taught history at Yale University, and is currently school professor of history and Leverhulme personal research professor at the London School of Economics and Political Science. A Fellow of the British Academy and a regular commentator on current events as well as past cultures, her most recent book is *Captives: Britain, Empire and the World 1600–1850* (2003). Her *Britons: Forging the Nation 1707–1837* (1992) won the Wolfson Prize and provoked a major debate on national identities in the UK and elsewhere. Previous books include *In Defiance of Oligarchy: The Tory Party 1714–1760* (1982) and *Namier* (1989).

16 Islam believes that Judaism, Christianity and Islam are all manifestations of the same religion.

17 Bryan Sykes, professor of genetics at the Institute of Molecular Medicine at Oxford University, and editor of *The Human Inheritance: Genes, Language, and Evolution* (1999), says that the human race has more in common than what superficially seems to separate it. Research by the Human Genome Project confirms that the human genome sequence is 99.9 per cent the same in all people.

18 Including the emperor Hadrian.

19 Research shows that long before 5000 BC Mesopotamian priesthoods held the mathematical secrets of building.

20 The esoteric philosophy of ancient Egypt is to be found in the body of writings known as the Trismegistic Book – named after the Egyptian deity Thoth, who was renamed Hermes Trismegistus by the Greeks.

21 The Great Pyramid in Egypt has four sides facing the four cardinal points of the compass. Stone circles, built at Stonehenge about 2200 BC, have axes aligned to the sun. The geometric proportions used in the building of Chartres, in common with other Gothic cathedrals, uses a proportion of 2:1 – the same proportions as the ground plan for the Temple of Solomon, although it is also said that the Temple of Solomon was actually an allegory for divine order.

22 An X-ray of fractal patterns in a beryl and the analysis of a mosque tile show the same geometric pattern.

23 A *muqarna* is an architectural component unique to Islamic architecture, in which niche-like components combine in successive layers to create surfaces in three-dimensional geometric compositions.

24 Fivefold geometry occurs regularly in Gothic architecture.

25 Christopher Wren said that both historical facts and structural evidence show that the origin of Gothic architecture lay in the Islamic. He called this the 'Saracenic Theory' (see Christopher Wren, the Junior (1675–1747), *Parentalia, or Memoirs of the Family of the Wrens*, viz Matthew Bishop, printed for T Osborn and R Dodsley (London), 1750). In St Paul's Cathedral, Wren adopted various Islamic architectural techniques, including the structure of the domes in the aisles, and the dome and tower combination and use of corner squinches (see Miles Danby, *Moorish Style*, Phaidon (London), 1995). See also F Gross (ed), *1808 Essays on Gothic Architecture by the Reverend T Wharton et al*, 3rd edn, 1731–91, J Taylor, at the Architectural Library in London.

26 Noam Chomsky, 'Market Democracy in a Neoliberal Order: Doctrines and Reality', Davie Lecture, University of Cape Town, South Africa, May 1997.

27 The Aga Khan Award for Architecture recognises examples of architectural excellence in areas such as contemporary design, social housing, restoration, environmental and landscape design, and community improvement in societies around the world in which Muslims have a significant presence.

28 Hebron, Palestine.

29 Tuwaiq Palace is a recreation centre for the diplomatic quarter in Riyadh.

30 Slum Networking, Indore.

31 The Alhamra Arts Council in Lahore.

32 The Vidhan Bhavan Madhya Pradesh State Assembly.

33 The Aga Khan is the spiritual leader of the Ismaili sect. Like the Sufis, the Ismailis say that theory remains sterile without spiritual achievement; the way of knowledge is none other than experiencing the knowledge received from an inspired, sincere and credible teacher, for we cannot achieve true understanding through reasoning about the Creator.

34 Robert Ivy, FAIA Editor in Chief, 'Interview with His Highness the Aga Khan', *Architectural Record*, 31 August, 2001. ∆

The Middle East and US Foreign Policy:
A
Personal
Perspective

Barbara Smith was both a writer and editor at *The Economist* for 47 years. Until her retirement in October 2003, she was the international editor for the Middle East and Africa, a position that brought her into contact with many major political figures in the Middle East. Here she gives her own insights into the widening chasm between the Arab world and the United States during the Bush administration.

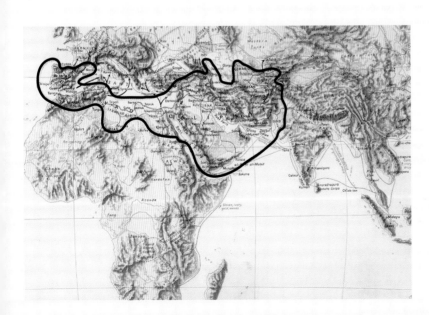

Map of the Islamic World *circa* AD 750
By 636 AD, the Muslims ruled Jerusalem, Damascus and Antioch; by 651 they had conquered Persia and moved west into Africa. In 646 they conquered Egypt and spread across northern Africa, and in 711 they invaded Spain. Islamic conquests continued during this period, through North Africa to Spain and France in the West, and to Sind, Central Asia and Transoxiana in the East. From their capital in Damascus, the Umayyad caliphate ruled a multicultural Islamic world, which stretched from the western borders of China to southern France. Although the caliphate had 'Arab' origins, the Islamic empires that followed were essentially non-Arab.

'Arabs and Americans are like ships passing in the night, sounding their horns, firing their guns, making known their views but having no impact on the other.'[1] So, recently, wrote Rami Khouri, the executive editor of the *Daily Star* in Beirut and a thoughtful commentator on Arab–Western relations. However, the image he describes isn't quite accurate, of course: the current US government's mighty battleship has been colliding, often and painfully, with the Arab world's sadly rudderless yacht, and the failure to communicate is crucial. The Bush administration's insistence on neat, explicit, black-and-white classifications of identities and aims, explains Mr Khouri, becomes lost amid the Middle East's tradition of multiple identities and sometimes hidden aims.

Since 11 September 2001, the Bush administration's policy towards the Middle East has been aimed, first, at achieving victory in America's war on 'terror' and, second, at applying a democratic make-up to the face of the Arab world.[2] The Arabs are not unsympathetic to these goals; their governments are engaged in police and intelligence activities to fight terrorism and some have gone as far as to jump on the American anti-terrorist bandwagon and brand domestic opponents – resistance fighters and separatists – as international terrorists. Moreover, the Arabs have become deeply conscious that their forms of governance are out of step with most other regions of the world and, indeed, with the 21st century. Thus, it is not the goals of us foreign policy that they oppose and deeply resent, but the high-handed and unilateralist manner in which America pursues those goals.

The Bush administration's claims of impunity, of being above the law – in other words, the assumption of the role of judge, jury and executioner – in the pursuit of 'terrorists' has antagonised the Arab people and, indeed, Asian Muslims too (only some 280 million of the world's 1.2 billion Muslims live in Arab countries, but the Arab world, for religious and historic reasons, remains the heartland of Islam). Despite President George Bush's denial that Islam was to blame for the atrocities of 11 September, his war on terror and on 'evil' has come, however wrongly, to be seen by many as a phenomenon that approaches the clash of Islamic and Western civilisations forecast by the writer Samuel Huntington, with Islamist militants representing Islam and the US championing the West.

In an article in the *Atlantic Monthly* (December 2003), George Soros, an American financier, sums up what he believes to be the underlying principles of current US foreign policy: 'Power prevails and law legitimises what prevails. The United States is unquestionably the dominant power ... and therefore is in a position to impose its views, interests and values. The world would benefit from adopting those values.' Earlier administrations failed to impose them, but President Bush believes that America must now, after the September 2001 terrorist attacks, find a way to assert its values and supremacy the world over.

The arrogance inherent in such principles would be resented whatever the circumstances: values can rarely, if ever, be imposed from outside. But the greater delusion is the idea that the motivation behind Muslim hostility towards the US is opposition to such Western values as freedom and democracy. The al-Qaida leaders may indeed find the modern Western way of life deeply distasteful, but opinion polls show that most Muslims, including Arabs, admire the basic values of freedom, tolerance and democracy.[3] They oppose not American values but American foreign policy: for example, America's invasion and occupation of Iraq and tacit support for Israel's occupation of Palestine.

Even al-Qaida's campaign against the US and its allies is driven, first and foremost, by a determination to resist Western influence over Arab and other Muslim countries. Osama bin Laden's call to arms was initially against US foreign policy in the Middle East: its troops in Saudi Arabia, its sanctions campaign against Iraq, its help for Israel and backing for the Egyptian regime. However, since 11 September the issues have become much sharper, with America's invasion of first Afghanistan and then Iraq, and with Israel freed from any American restraint in crushing the Palestinian resistance.

Bush's war on Iraq was a diversion from, or a blurring of, the war on terrorism: whatever the US government's reasons for invading Iraq, no link has ever been found between Saddam Hussein's regime and Osama bin Laden. But one result of this blurring is that the line between anti-American Islamist terrorism and resistance groups fighting for nationalist reasons is now less distinct than it was. With the occupation of Iraq having gone disastrously wrong for the Americans, at least in its initial phases, and with the violence still showing no sign of ending, anti-American feeling is now more fierce and more general. This animosity has not yet been calmed by the handing over of partial sovereignty to an interim Iraqi government.

Although the US government has never enjoyed greater or more unchallenged power in the world than it does today, it has rarely possessed so little influence, particularly in Muslim countries. A poll conducted in spring 2004 by the nonpartisan Pew Research Centre showed the strength of Muslim resentment across nine countries. In three of the four Muslim countries surveyed – Jordan, Pakistan and Morocco – the majority felt that the suicide bombings against Americans and other

Map of the Islamic World *circa* AD **1300**
From AD 750 onwards, for several centuries, the Abbasid caliphs ruled an empire greater in size than the imperial Roman realms. This vast, multiethnic Islamic world included Spain and represented one of the greatest flowerings of knowledge humanity has known. In 1492, the Muslims lost Spain, bringing nearly 800 years of Islamic rule in the Iberian Peninsula to an end.

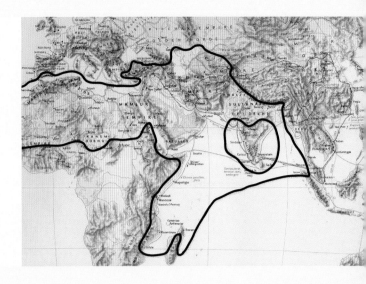

In three of the four Muslim countries surveyed – Jordan, Pakistan and Morocco – the majority felt that the suicide bombings against Americans and other Westerners in Iraq were justifiable, and even in Turkey as many as 31 per cent condoned such attacks. Only the Americans themselves, and a tiny majority of Britons, thought the motives behind the US-led war on terrorism were sincere; most believed it was an effort to dominate the world or control Middle Eastern oil.

Westerners in Iraq were justifiable, and even in Turkey as many as 31 per cent condoned such attacks. Only the Americans themselves, and a tiny majority of Britons, thought the motives behind the US-led war on terrorism were sincere; most believed it was an effort to dominate the world or control Middle Eastern oil. In addition, 65 per cent of people in Pakistan, and 55 per cent in Jordan, expressed favourable views of Osama bin Laden.

Arab scepticism and bitterness about Western motives is solidly based. It was, after all, the blandishments of Britain and France in the First World War that aroused the Arab world from centuries of political lethargy under the Ottoman Empire, recalling the years of ancient splendour when Europe was stuck in darkness and Arab learning shone brightly. The hope of independence was heady: the Arabs learnt about self-determination from the West, and dared to rebel against the Turks. But the Europeans were false friends, obeying the imperatives of an all-out war with little thought for what they were promising; for example, a national home for the Jews in Palestine.

Once the war was over, Britain and France failed to keep their promise to the Arabs in the Fertile Crescent (and were ambivalent, until the last moment, about their promise to the Jews). Instead, between them, they set up mandates and kingdoms that were, in effect, colonies in disguise, run by the British and French until the Arabs, one by one, rebelled. Many of the current borders still reflect the dictates of the former colonisers rather than local dispositions, leading to the necessary fabrication of new national identities[4] and frontiers; few would now choose to break up established states or allow separatist movements to thrive.

The imperialists' attitude to their charges was paternal or even patronising. Earl Cromer, consul-general in Egypt for about 15 years prior to the First World War, contrasted the oriental and occidental minds in a manner damning to the East. John Glubb, commander of Jordan's Foreign Legion from 1939 to 1956, wrote:

'We have given them self-government for which they are totally unfitted. They veer naturally towards dictatorship.' Indeed, with the imperialists gone, many of the new independent governments aped the old colonial administrations (rather than the governments behind these administrations), adopting the characteristics of centralisation, little separation of power between the different branches of government, and a generally paternalistic attitude.

The resented colonial past, and the sour British–French betrayal, are long gone. The establishment of Israel in the old Palestine mandate is also more than half a century past, but the unresolved grievances of the Palestinians who once lived there remains as fresh as yesteryear. The Arab world took a long time, and several bitter military defeats, to accept that Israel is here to stay. Basically, it is now prepared to recognise, and deal normally with, the state if Israel retreats to the land it held (78 per cent of the old mandate) before it swallowed up the rest of the territory in the traumatic 1967 war. Led by Saudi Arabia's Crown Prince Abdullah, the Arab League members have offered Israel full recognition and rights in return for allowing a Palestinian state in all of the West Bank and Gaza, including East Jerusalem. Israel's prime minister, Ariel Sharon, disdained the offer without even considering it.

Sharon is now proposing a unilateral withdrawal from Gaza, which includes dismantling all of the small Israeli settlements there, though he would retain the right to send the Israeli army back to the territory should violence emanate from Gaza. Far-right members of the Israeli government, and a majority in Sharon's own Likud party, oppose this move, but the prime minister seems determined to push it through. Hamas, the militant Islamic group in the occupied territories, and other military movements are treating Israel's possible retreat from Gaza as a victory, comparing it with Hezbollah's victory in driving the Israelis out of south Lebanon. However, many Palestinians are more sceptical; they see the Gaza move as a diversion from the West Bank, where the Palestinians are being squeezed into ever smaller segments between ever enlarging Israeli settlements. Gaza, crammed with two-time refugees, is wretchedly poor. Its workforce has had no option but to labour for Israel, and when Israel slammed the door, they became unemployed. Palestinians in the West Bank and Jerusalem joke bitterly: 'We will take back Gaza, but what will Sharon give us in return?'

Sharon has made it quite clear that he will not deal with the Palestinians until all terrorism, and other forms of violent resistance, are ended – and even then not on any sort of equal footing. Sharon's attitude to the Palestinians is, as it has always been, that they will eventually have no choice but to accept whatever Israel is prepared to offer them. This arrogant unilateralism is not entirely different from that of recent US foreign policy, though an exaggeration of it. Indeed, the policy of military pre-emption or anticipatory retaliation – of attacking before you are attacked – was Israel's long before the Bush administration adopted it.

The closeness of the current Israeli and US governments leaves the Arabs without a policy on Palestine. Sharon was in the business of transforming Palestinian militants into international terrorists even before the suicide bombing began in earnest. Now that it has, Palestinian terrorism has been blended into the 'war on terror', and the Israelis have carte blanche to deal with it. The Americans, it seems, will barely lift a finger to restrain them. Yet America's uncritical support for Israel is undoubtedly the biggest obstacle to its standing in the Arab world. When President Bush tries to urge the Arab governments towards certain policies, the answer is a speedy: 'Why put pressure on us, when what is needed is more pressure on Israel?' But Bush is not expected to exert any pressure at all on his ally in the war on terrorism – Sharon.

Without such pressure there is no hope of bringing the Israeli–Palestinian conflict to any peaceful conclusion. Instead, US foreign policy has looked to leapfrog over intractable issues by talking, in far grander terms, of what was at first called the 'Greater Middle East Initiative'. The original concept of this plan was, apparently, for the administration to 'look beyond immediate troublespots to institutionalise a policy of change for the region'. Or, to put it crudely, to remake the face of the Middle East, wiping off the old dictatorships, replacing them with reformed, democratic regimes. Liberty must take root throughout the Middle East if the region is to leave behind stagnation, tyranny and violence, proclaimed Bush's national security adviser, Condoleezza Rice, in March 2004.

The Arabs are aware of the need for change. Nearly two-thirds of the world's countries now enjoy electoral democracy to a greater or lesser degree, yet the 22 members of the Arab League do not. They remain almost uniformly oligarchic (though Lebanon is an exception, it has its own problems). No Arab leader has been peacefully ousted at the ballot box. The Arabs know that they are out of step with the rest of the world, and that this cannot continue.

But they do not want democracy to be imposed from outside. The American initiative became public in spring 2004, arousing great hostility in the Arab world. There was talk of the approach being modelled on the 1975

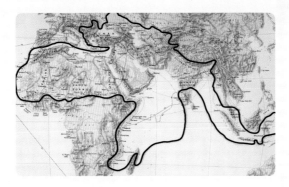

Map of the Islamic World *circa* AD 1500

In 1453, the Turkish Ottomans conquered Constantinople. From 1520 until 1566, Sultan Süleyman presided over the most powerful empire in the world, and a diversity of peoples that included populations of the Middle Eastern regions and the Balkan Peninsula. To the immediate east lay Safavid Persia, which coexisted with Central Asian Islamic khanates. Further east, the Mogul Empire linked India to the larger Islamic world. And still further east, Islamic kingdoms in Southeast Asia contained diverse peoples in Malaysia, southern Thailand, Indonesia, Brunei and the southern Philippines. In Africa, Muslim sultanates existed in Mali, Timbucktu in West Africa, and Harar in East Africa. Though there were fluctuations in the borders between the various Islamic empires, on the whole Islamic empires created a good measure of stability for many centuries. Collapse of this stability in the mid-18th century opened the way for the intervention of European powers.

Helsinki accords which, with their emphasis on human rights and fundamental freedoms, and their monitoring systems, are thought to have contributed to the collapse of communist regimes in Europe. To counter this hostility, the Americans presented a watered-down version of the initiative in June to the G8 meeting of industrialised countries, the new proposal concentrating on economic development and allowing Arab involvement in the human-rights monitoring system to be voluntary.

In fact, America's initiative is largely based on the Arabs' own ideas. In 2002 the UN Development Programme published the first in a hard-hitting series on Arab human development. Written by Arab scholars, this challenged the Arab world to overcome three cardinal obstacles to human development in the region: the severe and widening gaps in knowledge, political freedom and women's empowerment. A second report published in 2004 concentrated on 'knowledge', or the lack of it: the current state of learning and intellectual enquiry in the Arab world.

It is generally agreed that the Arab region is in a bad way, suffering from a surfeit of autocratic rulers, and from the world's highest rates of unemployment and population growth. There is a paradox of stable and enduring regimes and deeply disturbed societies.

Islam, as Albert Hourani wrote in his history of the Arabs, has long provided the language of opposition to Western power and influence, to corrupt and ineffective governments, and to a society that seems to have lost its moral direction. Movements such as the Muslim Brotherhood,

led by articulate and educated men, had great appeal among the masses, forcing governments to move towards the general Islamisation of society. And the threat of an Islamist takeover had many governments trembling in the years after the 1979 Islamic Revolution in Iran.

This threat had largely disappeared – until it was violently reborn in its new anti-American format. Fear of the new–old phenomenon has driven some US writers to warn of a Middle East that is no less than a cauldron of hate and obscurantism. Of course, it is nothing like that. But with the new violence of militant fundamentalist movements, the Bush administration's high-handedness, the cruel chaos in post-Saddam Iraq, the wobbliness of a few regimes and the unending horrors of the Israeli–Palestine conflict, the Middle East is certainly in trouble.

The notion that the US has an exemplary national mission has always been central to American thought. But can it really transform the stubborn Arab world? A look at the violence in Iraq, and the stalemate in Palestine, provides an answer, of sorts, to this question. The Arabs, and indeed the Muslim world beyond, do indeed need America's help. But they do not need it in the way that, under President George Bush, it has been proffered. ∆

Notes
1 'The US public diplomacy hoax: Why do they keep insulting us?', *Daily Star* (Beirut), 11 February 2004.
2 The Bush doctrine was first aired in a presidential speech at West Point in June 2002, and incorporated three months later into the National Security Strategy. Veiled in double-speak, it has two main principles: the United States will do everything in its power to maintain its unquestioned military supremacy, and the United States has the right to pre-emptive action. The doctrine establishes two kinds of sovereignty: the sovereignty of the United States, which takes precedence over international treaties and obligations, and the lesser sovereignty of other states. There is an evident contradiction between the Bush administration's idea of freedom and democracy and the actual principles and requirements of freedom and democracy. In a free society, people define democracy for themselves, but the Bush administration sets out to create 'democracies'. Iraq demonstrates the counterproductive nature of the Bush doctrine. The Council on Foreign Relations has produced three national-security strategy options: first, the pursuit of American supremacy through the Bush doctrine of pre-emptive military action, as advocated by the neo-conservatives; second, the continuation of the earlier US policy of deterrence and containment, supported by Colin Powell and the moderate wings of both parties; and the third option, which looks to the US government to lead visionary multilateral efforts via constructive action – for example, collective security, fairer trade rules and nonviolation of the sovereignty of others. This last approach has no support from any official group.
3 Democracy is a modern, 20th-century phenomenon with universal appeal. Freedom and democracy are universal and not just 'American' values. Arab thinkers, from political analysts and commentators, such as Mohammad Hassanein Heikal and the late Edward Said, to writers in the mainstream Arab press, are in no doubt about their belief in, and longing for, freedom and democracy. There are many reasons why the Arab world is so undemocratic but, among Arabs, there is a feeling that it is at least partly due to the US government's promotion of its own interests, and its support of undemocratic and corrupt leaders.
4 Iraq, Jordan and Lebanon are new identities, invented in the 20th century by colonial interests. The present-day United Arab Emirates were sheikhdoms along the Gulf Coast. In 1820, the British fleet arrived in the Gulf, destroyed the nine sheikhdoms of the Qawasim tribal confederation, imposed a general treaty of peace and installed a garrison. In order to keep France and Russia out, Britain established a protectorate over the 'Trucial Coast' in 1892. The first oil concessions were granted in 1939. Negotiations eventually led, in 1971, to the independence of Bahrain and Qatar and the formation of new identities – the United Arab Emirates.

Islamic Architecture as a Field of Historical Enquiry

For many years, Islamic architecture, as a field of historical enquiry, was hampered by its Orientalist roots. Architectural forms were classified by types and styles, and perceived as sedate, static and unevolving. **Nasser Rabbat**, Aga Khan Professor of Islamic Architecture at MIT, demonstrates a dynamic way forward for the discipline.

Islamic architecture, long labelled with inaccurate and controversial qualifiers such as 'Saracenic', 'Moorish' or 'Mohammedan' was, until recently, among the least theoretically developed areas of enquiry in the field of architecture.[1] Few studies existed that moved beyond the taxonomic, typological or stylistic framework on the one hand, or the religiously or culturally essentialist or environmentally deterministic on the other. These approaches reflected the enduring influence of the two major and interdependent scholarly traditions that dominated the development of the study of the history of Islamic architecture since its inception until the late 20th century. The first stemmed from the peculiar historiography of the study of Islam in the West that came to be called Orientalism, and its various peregrinations both in the West and in the Islamic world. The second was the authoritative historiography of art and architectural history which, until the 1980s, routinely portrayed the history of Western architecture as history of architecture *par excellence*, while casting the architecture of other cultures in anthropological and ahistorical categories.[2]

The pioneering students of Islamic architecture were almost all European architects, artists and draughtspeople who, from as early as the 1820s, travelled to the 'Orient' in the wake of the first European military interventions

in search of adventure, employment and the fantasy associated with this long-mysterious land. Some worked for individual patrons who sponsored expeditions and study tours either as an aristocratic recreation or for profit. Others worked for local or colonial authorities, which were concurrently spreading their dominion in the various regions of the Islamic world and needed the services of all classes of specialists to establish and maintain a new order in their territorial possessions. And still others worked for universities or learned societies in the West that were interested in the architecture of specific areas or periods for scholarly or religious reasons.

Like Orientalists in various other fields of enquiry, the early students of Islamic architecture became engaged in the vast enterprise of collecting, processing and interpreting data on all aspects of culture and society in the Orient. They visited Oriental cities and sites (primarily in Spain, western Turkey, the Holy Land and Egypt), measured and recorded buildings and ruins, and illustrated these using all sorts of techniques from freehand sketches to exact camera lucida projections. They also ferreted through the limited available written sources to verify the historical details about the structures: date, provenance, patron, cost and the like. They then produced impressive catalogues of series of buildings, singular monuments, and architectural and ornamental details that began to introduce to Europe, and to the dominant classes in the Orient itself, the rich Islamic architectural heritage that was hitherto almost totally unknown.[3]

The trailblazers were followed by several generations of architects, draughtspeople and, ultimately, archaeologists, who expanded the scope of the survey to Anatolia, Persia, India, Morocco and Arabia, and eventually penetrated the faraway reaches of the Islamic world, such as Central Asia or sub-Saharan Africa. Although most of the surveyors were still European, natives of the Islamic world began to participate in the process from as early as the first decade of the 20th century. Before the middle of the century, the terrain had been mostly mapped out, and with the nagging exception of Southeast Asia, most major buildings in the Islamic world had been measured, recorded and classified into types and styles following a rather rigid dynastic periodisation, which is still with us today.

But despite their erudite and prodigious output, most early students were neither equipped to, nor interested in, communicating the substantial intracultural variety and purposeful continuity within Islamic architecture, nor its conscious interaction with the architecture of other cultures, past and present. Instead, they set the stage for a self-contained architectural discourse charting the history of Islamic architecture as an endogenous and, seemingly, insular tradition that began with the building of the Mosque of the Prophet in Medina around AD 620, and inexplicably fizzled out with the dawn of the colonial age in the late 18th century.

This trajectory was academically and disciplinarily formalised when Islamic architecture finally became a subject of study of art history. This happened slowly and gradually in the early part of the 20th century with the establishment of the first academic chairs for the study of Islamic art history, which included architectural history, in Western universities and research centres. The hegemonic conceptual framework of Western art history, which had its roots in the late 18th-century German and French theories of art, framed the intricate network of epistemological and cultural conventions that produced and used art historical knowledge. It also constituted the only system via which an area of study could gain legitimacy within art history. Moreover, it controlled the scope and methods of all subdisciplines, including Islamic architecture, and assigned them their slots in a chronologically, geographically and even ideologically prescribed hierarchy.[4]

Accordingly, Islamic architecture was reduced to a set of prevalent characterisations – static, sensual and ornamental being the favourite among them – that stood in stark contrast to the self-conscious and historically evolving attributes frequently portrayed as specific to Western architecture. Instances that did not fit into this division – for example, the shared classical heritage in the medieval Middle East and Europe, the fruitful interaction between them during the Crusades, and their similar historicising stances in the 18th century – were explained away as oddities or aberrations provoked by singular historical circumstances.

The limitations of this burdensome, scholarly lineage were not seriously challenged until the 1980s. Empowered by critical developments in cultural studies after the publication of Edward Said's seminal book *Orientalism* in 1978, students of Islamic architecture began to question the validity of using geographic, historical, religious and cultural boundaries as disciplinary frameworks. They also began to hesitantly, yet exuberantly, ease into the liberating space of theory and method, and to extend their domain of enquiry into hitherto neglected periods, areas and points of contact with other cultures. The notions of uniformity, introversion, and cultural and religious determinism that long dominated the study of Islamic architecture

Above
The main *iwan* (archway) in the madrasah of Sultan Qalawun in Cairo (1284), a curious example of a basilical composition inserted inside an *iwan*.

began to lose their grip as more and more scholars turned to the multiculturalist method in their enquiry. Some focused on the intercultural development of Islamic architecture over the last 15 centuries, with its substantial connections to the Late Antique Mediterranean, Iranian and Hindu–Buddhist cultures in the early periods and the European, Asian and African cultures of recent times.[5] Others began to dip into the intracultural spaces – that is, zones within a given society at a given time that are shared by its diverse constituent groups – where people have always met and exchanged ideas, views, beliefs and practices and, in the process, created architecture.

Thus, the contributions of the various Islamic fringe sects and esoteric religious orders, Christian and Jewish denominations, Zoroastrians, Buddhists, Hindus and others have started to be analysed as both instrumental components of a shared architectural language and as distinct expressions within its fold. The cumulative effect of these critical and revisionist enquiries has been to set Islamic architecture well on its way to finally devising its own epistemological and methodological contours, which will undoubtedly enrich both

Dynastic periodisation has also resulted in needlessly privileging the role of the patrons in the conception of architecture and its signification to the detriment of the designers and builders. In the same way, categorising Islamic architecture after the Western stylistic sequence — classical, medieval or Baroque — has subjected the development of Islamic architecture to the rhythm of another architectural tradition, though the two have only intermittently shared the same trajectory.

the discipline and practice of architecture in the Islamic world and beyond.

Three main issues can be singled out as promising venues in the field's current quest for critical research programmes. First is a claim for a dynamic historical framework. Piggybacking on other historical frameworks and other periodisations has clearly distorted the understanding of Islamic architecture for far too long. For example, classifying Islamic architecture along the dynastic sequence of Islamic history – that is, to speak of Abbasid or Mamluk architecture – has led to the disregard for the architecture's autonomous evolution, since artistic and architectural movements rarely correspond to political shifts. Dynastic periodisation has also resulted in needlessly privileging the role of the patrons in the conception of architecture and its signification to the detriment of the designers and builders. In the same way, categorising Islamic architecture after the Western stylistic sequence – classical, medieval or Baroque – has subjected the development of Islamic architecture to the rhythm of another architectural tradition, though the two have only intermittently shared the same trajectory. This has also meant that some attributes of Islamic architecture have been glossed over when they were named after formally, or conceptually, comparable characteristics of Western architecture, of which Baroque Ottoman is the most conspicuous, even though the similarity was mostly skin-deep and historically unsubstantiated.

This terminological confusion has pervaded Islamic architecture to the point that any serious revision of the methods and conceptual frameworks of the field have to begin with a critical analysis of chronological division and historical parallels. Furthermore, as any cursory historical investigation will demonstrate, other decisive forces – such as massive population movements, lingering national and tribal pride, theological and spiritual breakthroughs, not to speak of artistic, structural and technological innovations – had a more profound effect on architecture in Islamic history than mere dynastic change. But this does not mean that dynastic nomenclature has to be totally thrown out. Some terms seem to be reasonably fitting, especially when applied to the specific geographic area where a truly dynastic architecture flourished, for example Umayyad or Seljuk architecture.

In other instances, different designations need to be devised either because several dynasties followed the same artistic paradigm – as in the case of the various splinter dynasties in the early Abbasid period, or the post-Seljukid small princedoms in Anatolia and Syria – or a stylistic or typological rupture occurred in mid-dynastic reign. It is very difficult, for example, to pinpoint the difference in the architecture of the two successive dynasties, Ayyubids and Mamluks, in Cairo, although, otherwise, they were politically and socially particularly distinct. A flexible and multireferential periodisation, with chronologically open-ended boundaries that account for the stylistic, dynastic and sociocultural overlaps, would provide the most adequate historical setting for the study of Islamic architecture.

A second topic to explore is what can be called the multicultural quality of Islamic architecture, a quality shared by all architectural traditions with a living history. No single model – or unique cultural reference for that matter – can be induced as the sole inspiration behind any of the famous examples of Islamic architecture. Different tensions were at work. The people and groups concerned seem to have adopted, borrowed, resurrected and invented at every stage, and then reapplied the new creative process to the next work. The buildings they constructed reflected these choices in their forms, spaces and techniques, but also exhibited a relative stability of their intentions and goals. They referred to multifarious cultures, traditions, ideals and images which their patrons, designers and builders considered suitable, representative or desirable, for themselves and for their cultures.

The multicultural quality, however, goes beyond colouring our perception of Islamic architecture to conditioning the means by which we can analyse it. Thus, not only were divergences from a putative norm common, but the very idea of an overarching conformism or an underlying essentialism do not seem to provide an adequate explanation for any of the bold and innovative buildings dotting the historical landscape across the Islamic world. Old research models will have to be abandoned and new methods designed to comprehend and structure the diverse alignments that have asserted, and reasserted, themselves in diverse and flexible combinations within the domain of Islamic architecture throughout its long history.

Some experiments seem to have led to nowhere, and were dropped either immediately or after a few trials. Others were felt to be more satisfactory and were adopted for longer stretches of time. And still others became cultural standards, used over and over again, some even surviving the 'pre-Modern' periods to become iconic markers in the revival of 'Islamic architecture' as a design category pursued by many practitioners today. The cases of the arch and dome as carriers of cultural meanings are such examples. Not only did they complete the transition into modern times with hardly a change in their significance, but their use has

expanded to permeate all religious structures built by Muslims in the last century.

A third critical issue, and one concomitant with the second point, is the dialogic dimension discernible in Islamic architecture. In many of its celebrated examples, this architecture appears to have been guided by a purposeful intellectual and aesthetic exchange within its own multicultural environment or with past and contemporary cultures near and far. Thus, Islamic architecture has interlocutors in Late Antique, Persian, South Arabian, Syriac, Coptic, Visigothic, Byzantine, Armenian, Buddhist and Hindu architectural traditions, and recently Modern and Postmodern European ones. But rather than mimetic, the process seems to have been dialogic; that is, it went beyond one-way copying to consciously engage the other architectural traditions in an interchange that resulted in original yet historically and territorially grounded architecture. This is evident in all Umayyad structures known to us today.[6] But it is also apparent in a vast array of other examples where the cultural dialogue has visibly modified the formal outcome. These include medieval Persian and Central Asian tomb towers; Seljukid and pre-Ottoman Anatolian mosques, madrasahs and *tekkes* (charitable structures serving Sufis); Egyptian, Syrian and North African palaces with basilical plans; Ghurid, Mamluk and Tughluqid architecture in India; and some recent modernistically sensible mosques such as the White Mosque of Visoko or the Parliament Mosque in Ankara, to list but a few.

The effects of this dialogic exchange on the other cultural interlocutors were as pervasive as they were

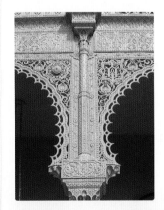

Right and opposite
The so-called Emir Saltuk Tomb
(end of 12th century) in Erzrum,
Turkey (right), a magnificent
and unique example of multi-
level dialogue with several
architectural traditions –
Soghdian Central Asian,
Anatolian Armenian and
Byzantine, and possibly late
Romanesque, and (opposite)
the Grand National Assembly
Mosque in Ankara (1985–9),
designed by the Çinici team;
a bold adoption of modernistic
gestures to the construction
of the most traditional of Islamic
architectural types – the
congregational mosque.

on Islamic architecture, despite the dominant art-historical framework that tends to ignore such exchanges and discourage any serious investigation into their scope and significance. Young scholars working on Byzantine, medieval European, Eastern Christian and Hindu architectural traditions are coming up with countless instances of direct and evidently conscious and intentional adaptations from Islamic architectural sources.[7]

Thus, to begin to critically understand the history of Islamic architecture, it is no longer adequate to study only its particular material, conceptual, social or religious contexts. Nor is it sufficient simply to identify its intra- or extra-cultural references and to decipher the various channels of appropriation they have traversed. The enquiry itself must be recast to account for the decisive role of intellectual and disciplinary dialogue in the emergence and evolution of the variegated architectural traditions that we today call Islamic. This interpretation shifts the focus from passive to dynamic exchange, and introduces the notions of reception, translation and representation in reading and explaining the unfolding of Islamic architecture as an active and contributive component of world architecture. It also offers a methodologically solid framework to consider how an open-ended search for expressive forms and designs has endowed Islamic architecture, like other major architectural traditions everywhere, with a vibrant historical self-consciousness.

Obviously, this conclusion stands in stark contrast to the defamed Orientalist view that identifies Islamic architecture with sedate, static and supra-historical forms, which has unfortunately and, possibly unwittingly, been resurrected by some of the contemporary essentialist theoreticians and practitioners looking for easily definable or loudly expressive architecture. ⌂

Notes
1 Two recent surveys of the field make this clear: see Stephen Vernoit, 'Islamic art and architecture: an overview of scholarship and collecting, c 1850–c 1950', in Stephen Vernoit (ed), *Discovering Islamic Art: Scholars, Collectors and Collections 1850–1950*, B Tauris (London), 2000, pp 1–61; Sheila S Blair and Jonathan M Bloom, 'The mirage of Islamic art: reflections on the study of an unwieldy field', *Art Bulletin* 85, 1, March 2003, pp 152–84.
2 The most graphic illustration of this division is Sir Banister Fletcher's 'Tree of Architecture', which clearly assigns to non-Western architectural traditions, called nonhistorical styles, dead-end branches while preserving the trunk, and growing branches to Western or historical styles. The tree occupied the frontispiece of the first 16 editions of the book *A History of Architecture on the Comparative Method for the Student, Craftsman, and Amateur*, published between 1896 and 1961. For a critical discussion of Fletcher's dichotomous structure, see: Gulsum Baydar Nalbantoglu, 'Toward postcolonial openings: rereading Sir Banister Fletcher's History of Architecture', *Assemblage* 35, 1998, pp 6–17.
3 The most remarkable among these early studies are Pascal-Xavier Coste, *Architecture Arabe ou Monuments du Kaire mésurés et dessinés de 1818 à 1826* , Firmin-Didot (Paris) 1839; Girault de Prangey, *Souvenirs de Grenade et de l'Alhambra: monuments arabes et moresques de Cordoue, Séville et Grenade, dessinés et mesurés en 1832 et 1833,* Veith et Hauser (Paris), 1837; idem, *Essai sur l'architecture des Arabes et des Mores, en Espagne, en Sicile, et en Barbarie,* A Hauser (Paris), 1841; Owen Jones and Jules Goury, *Plans, Elevations, Sections and Details of the Alhambra from Drawings taken on the Spot in 1834 & 1837,* Owen Jones (London), 1852; Prisse d'Avennes, *L'art arabe d'aprés les monuments du Kaire depuis le VIIe siècle jusqu'á la fin du XVIIIe,* A Morel et cie (Paris), 1877.
4 See Zeynep Celik's discussion, 'Colonialism, Orientalism, and the Canon', *Art Bulletin* 78, 2, June 1996, pp 202–5. For a specific aspect see Nasser Rabbat, 'Writing the history of Islamic architecture of Cairo', *Design Book Review* 31, winter 1994, pp 48–51.
5 The list is becoming quite long. A selection of the variety of approaches and areas includes: RA Jairazbhoy, 'The Taj Mahal in the context of East and West: study in the comparative method', *Journal of the Warburg Courtauld Institute* 24, 1961, pp 59–88; Patrick Connor, *Oriental Architecture in the West*, Thames and Hudson (London), 1979; Gulru Necipoglu, 'Süleyman the Magnificent and the representation of power in the context of Ottoman-Hapsburg-papal rivalry', *Art Bulletin* 71, 3, September 1989, pp 401–27; Sibel Bozdogan, 'Journey to the East: Ways of looking at the Orient and the question of representation', *Journal of Architectural Education* 41, 4, summer 1988, pp 38–45; Cynthia Robinson, 'Mudéjar revisited: A prolegomenon to the reconstruction of perception, devotion and experience at the Mudéjar convent of Clarisas, Tordesillas, Spain (14th Century AD)', *RES43*, spring 2003, pp 51–77.
6 See Nasser Rabbat, 'The dialogic dimension in Umayyad art', *RES43*, spring 2003, pp 78–94.
7 See, for instance, Jerrilynn D Dodds, *Architecture and Ideology in Early Medieval Spain*, Pennsylvania State University Press, 1990; Finbarr B Flood, 'Pillars, palimpsests, and princely practices: Translating the past in Sultanate Delhi', *RES43*, spring 2003, pp 95–116; Michael W Mesiter, 'Crossing lines: architecture in early Islamic South Asia', *RES43,* spring 2003, pp 117–30.

Thus, to begin to critically understand the history of Islamic architecture, it is no longer adequate to study only its particular material, conceptual, social or religious contexts. Nor is it sufficient simply to identify its intra- or extracultural references and to decipher the various channels of appropriation they have traversed.

Defining Architecture

Rejecting the notion of a universal Islamic architecture, **Suha Özkan**, secretary-general of the Aga Khan Award for Architecture, espouses the great diversity and adaptive qualities that can be found in architecture appropriate to traditional Islamic communities throughout the world.

In the history and literature of architecture, there is a whole sector of the built environment that has erroneously, yet consistently, been referred to as 'Islamic architecture'. This qualification of architecture by faith does not hold valid for Christian, Buddhist or Hindu architecture. While in these other faiths only temples and churches are seen as religious architecture, for Islam all buildings, especially those of the past, are called Islamic.

Can a faith be the sole criterion by which architecture can be categorised? Absolutely not. Faiths are central to people's personal and social lives and behaviour. Architecture constitutes only a part of their role in the cultural realm. It is necessary to look further into the matter in order to understand the phenomenon of what is called 'Islamic architecture'.

Traditionally, the architecture developed within the context of the Muslim faith is effective as an important aspect of culture, defining and determining how people live and relate to each other and to their urban environment. The impenetrable, almost exclusive, privacy of the home and its strictly controlled access and visibility from the public realm of the town is perhaps a basic issue that defines all urban architecture. Furthermore, while certain common measures are required to provide comfortable and habitable spaces for the climatic conditions that prevail in almost all Arabic Muslim communities, we must not forget that only 15 per cent of Muslims are Arabs and live in hot, arid climates. Therefore it would be wrong to claim the validity of a universal Islamic architecture, or to base this claim exclusively on Arab architecture.

At the level of artistry, engineering and sophistication, the development of architecture in Islamic cultures through history has been comparable with the best of accomplishments elsewhere in the world. The most revered Renaissance architecture of the West finds its counterpart in the Islamic world. Who would claim that the Taj Mahal in Agra, the Sultan Hassan Mosque and Madrasah in Cairo or the Süleymaniye Mosque in Istanbul are the products of a lesser architectural expertise than St Peter's in Rome?

The strength of Islamic architecture has arisen not only from the intrinsic cultural values of the societies that generated it, but also from the fact that Islam has adapted itself in interacting with other cultures as it has spread. Noteworthy examples of such interaction are the interface between the Ottomans and the Eastern

OHO Joint Venture (Atelier Frei Otto/Buro Happold/Omrania), Tuwaiq Palace, Riyadh, Saudi Arabia, 1985
Recipient of the Aga Khan Award for Architecture, 1998
A daring confrontation between tradition, landscape and high technology, the building, for the Arriyadh Development Authority, covers 24,000 square metres, refers to two local archetypes – the fortress and the tent – and incorporates the natural phenomenon of oasis. Tuwaiq Palace takes its name from the 800-kilometre-long central Arabian escarpment that runs 50 kilometres west of Riyadh, and is a centre for festivals, meetings and official and social gatherings for the community at large. Set within a dramatic landscape, the building is enclosed by inclined curved walls, forming a sinuous curvilinear spine 800 metres long, 12 metres high and between 7 and 13 metres wide.

Mushrooming from the spine are tents supported by tensile-structure technology. The tents enclose the large-scale spaces: main lounges, reception areas, multipurpose halls, restaurants and a café. The landscape plan provides a dramatic contrast between the lush greenery of the outdoor spaces enclosed by the spine, and the arid rocky plateau beyond its walls. Reinforced concrete, and steel masts and cables, are the basic structural materials of the building. The white tents are made of Teflon-coated, woven-fibre fabric. Those facing the garden are of cable nets coated with custom-made, glazed blue ceramic tiles fastened to timber battens. Glass walls enclose the tents.

The structure is the product of an alliance between Omrania Architects, Planners and Engineers of Riyadh, Atelier Frei Otto of Germany and the UK structural engineering firm Büro Happold.

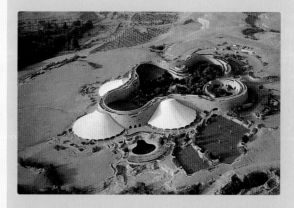

Opposite
Abdel Wahed El-Wakil, Corniche Mosque, Jeddah, Saudi Arabia, 1986
Recipient of the Aga Khan Award for Architecture, 1989
Of the present, and yet inspired by the past, this mosque, for the Municipality of Jeddah and Ministry of Pilgrimage and Endowments, is one of three set as pavilions along the corniche of Jeddah, facing the Red Sea. Classically Islamic in form, the mosque is contemporary in its intent. The construction is based on the architect's research on Egyptian building methods. The structure is brick coated with plaster, except for the dome interior, which has exposed bricks painted a dark bronze colour. The prayer hall is at the centre of a composition that includes the mihrab, projecting outwards from the eastern wall just below an oculus, an entrance porch covered by a catenary vault and a square-based minaret with an octagonal shaft.

Roman Empire or Byzance and the indigenous local cultures of today's Indonesia and Malaysia with what preceded them. These exchanges have been in the total realm of cultural tranformation that did not exclude architectural expressions. In the contemporary world of Islam, the same interaction is even more strongly evident. Now the massive cultural exchange is

between the Islamic world and the West. The challenge is 'modernity'.

Modernity as a way of life, and Modernism as an architectural revolution, have affected lives and cultural expressions worldwide, and cultures under Islam have naturally not been indifferent to these changes. The overwhelming transformations of the modern era, especially during the prosperous decades following the end of the Second World War, have had both positive and negative aspects that have altered not only our lives but also the built environment.

Since the beginning of the 20th century, Modernism has enshrined itself within two slogan-like assertions: Adolf Loos's 'Ornament is crime' and Louis Sullivan's 'Form follows function'. Addressing the aesthetics of industry and mass production, Modernism developed in leaps and bounds and became the uncontested lingua franca of architecture. It manifested itself in many art forms and became politically synonymous with being 'progressive'. Modernist architecture demanded simple, functional, industrially producible, sublime and honest expressions in built form.

With the pervasive use of reinforced concrete, which became abundant and inexpensively available, whole townscapes changed all over the world. In countries where building activity was regulated, this did not necessarily disfigure the environment with buildings devoid of any architectural value or significance. But elsewhere, lack of controls and an urgent need for new housing and other buildings meant that informal building activities became widespread. Speculative building practices abused the simplicity professed by Modernism and, eventually, bad and insensitive building practices were categorised as 'Modern architecture'. Even though it is unfair to blame Modernism for the worldwide spread of uniform, tedious and uninteresting buildings and urban environments built mainly for profit, Modernism has been seen by many to promulgate a set of values and premises that fails to respect cultural identity, historical continuity and climatic relevance.

The reaction against Modernism has taken many forms. Postmodernism, with its shallow ethics, was short-lived. Unlike Modernism, which expressed itself in many fields, including painting, sculpture, music, dance and industry, Postmodernism emerged within architecture and spread to other fields rather thinly, most notably literature, which it enhanced to a high

> The reaction against Modernism has taken many forms. Postmodernism, with its shallow ethics, was short-lived. Unlike Modernism, which expressed itself in many fields, including painting, sculpture, music, dance and industry, Postmodernism emerged within architecture and spread to other fields rather thinly, most notably literature, which it enhanced to a high degree. The Postmodern movement was endlessly preoccupied with superficial reflection of meaning, historical references and personal expression.

degree. The Postmodern movement was endlessly preoccupied with superficial reflection of meaning, historical references and personal expression.

Alternatively, the 'architecture of freedom' became a widespread denial of any form of control. It was a denial of political and planning control over building practices by people who took the initiative to solve their own housing problems. This movement based its discourse on everyday construction, generating vast settlements such as *favelas* and *barrios* in South America, *bastis* in the Indian subcontinent, *prosphikas* in Greece, *bidonvilles* in North Africa, *kampungs* in Indonesia and *gecekondus* in Turkey – all of them emerging after the Second World War as 'peoples' solutions' for housing in fast-urbanising countries. Recognition that this way of building offered solutions that challenged institutional or, for that matter, Modern architecture's failure to deal with demand found its catchphrase in John FC Turner's term 'Freedom to build'.

In almost every city in the Muslim world, the rapid sprawl of thoughtless and unplanned housing through the urban tissue after the 1950s instilled feelings of surprise and helplessness in architects and decision-makers alike. Spontaneous housing types were attributed the popular local names cited above. In addition, 'refugee camps' for displaced populations became important settlement types that Muslim communities had to confront. Architectural theory, practice and education not only disapproved of this form of building activity, but also entirely excluded and ignored it. In fact, when the Aga Khan Award for Architecture embraced and recognised improved conditions in such settlements as essential components of contemporary society, there was a public outcry. However, the award's pioneering decisions later met with esteem.

Third, and perhaps the most serious of the reactions against Modernism, is 'vernacularism'. Of the many aspects that have placed vernacularism critically at the centre of architectural theory, the most important are research into vernacular architecture and the revitalisation of traditional building practices.

Fast-growing cities have exerted enormous pressure on the historical fabric of their old towns by adopting cheap and inferior construction techniques with little concern for urban planning and development. Subsequently, new, transient and underprivileged groups have moved to these areas. Traditionally, such

Abdel Wahed El-Wakil, Halawa House, Agamy, Egypt, 1975
Recipient of the Aga Khan Award for Architecture, 1980
The house, for Esmat Ahmed Halawa of Cairo, consistently uses traditional methods of construction to satisfy contemporary needs. Based on traditional Islamic or Egyptian prototypes, in addition to the courtyard and its fountain, the house uses a courtyard plan, domes, vaults and arches, the articulation of space and sensitive use of light. It also has a loggia, a wind catch, alcoves, masonry benches and a belvedere. Except for the master mason, plasterer and carpenter, who were skilled craftspeople, local unskilled Bedouins carried out all other labour. The vaults and arches were constructed by the 'inclined arch' system without shuttering. The walls and roof provide good insulation, sunlight filters through *mashrabiyyas*, and the courtyard – which is in shade throughout the day – draws fresh sea air down through the wind catch. The paving materials play their part; the marble in the living areas is cool, and the Muqattam stone used outdoors gives a surface that can be walked on with bare feet even at the height of summer. The house represents a search for identity with traditional forms.

populations have had a lesser sense of a 'history of place' in urban areas and fewer economic means to cope with the deterioration of the historical heritage. At the same time, many international agencies whose mandate has been to conserve the historical heritage have been primarily preoccupied with monuments; they did not pay particular attention to the urban fabric of old towns until as late as the 1970s. In many cities, historical housing exists alongside monuments, forming a rich and varied urban fabric, but one that is fragile. Revitalisation requires not only architectural restoration but also social and economic infrastructure to ensure the survival and vitality of communities.

Housing has always been a central concern in architecture, and there has been a vast and increasing demand for new housing. In the best examples, families and individuals are embraced by architecture in its most personal sense. In any architectural discourse, this needs to be explored, especially by focusing on efforts directed at lower-income groups, be they public or private initiatives. Not enough successful projects have been recognised thus far, but there have been several important accomplishments.

Many Muslim communities live in rural conditions. However, rural development and the architecture appropriate to it have not figured in the mainstream of architecture. In architectural discourse, the undeniable

A commitment to ensuring the continuing relevance of building traditions has not been limited to revitalising historical buildings and urban fabric. Encouragement of vernacular building types and technologies that have been developed and transferred from one generation to the next also secures the continuity of building traditions.

importance of rural life and development must be stressed. In the rural context, development must be combined with environmental conservation. It is important that ingenious credit mechanisms are put in place to fund rural housing projects. And such projects must develop a humble but meaningful architectural language with simple construction techniques, while also improving living conditions, harvesting water, providing more time for the young – particularly girls and young women – to receive education, and providing means to reduce malnutrition. All these requirements can be achieved by simple but effective solutions from architects.

Mosque architecture should be viewed at many complex levels, and the different approaches that reflect the spirit of Islam and its temporal and geographic plurality need to be identified. There are many solutions and architectural expressions, including those that continue

vernacular traditions, those that express popular tastes, those that offer classical reinterpretations and those that represent modern creativity.

A commitment to ensuring the continuing relevance of building traditions has not been limited to revitalising historical buildings and urban fabric. Encouragement of vernacular building types and technologies that have been developed and transferred from one generation to the next also secures the continuity of building traditions.

Traditionalism in architecture cannot be discussed without considering the work of the Egyptian architect and activist Hassan Fathy, who challenged Modernism single-handedly. Fathy's multifaceted discourse and influence have given him an almost saintly status in the world of architecture, even though he did not enjoy a similar degree of success or recognition for his built work. His honesty and determination have made him a hero for generations of architects who have social concerns in architecture.

Fathy's beliefs and commitment to architecture are part of an endless battle that has continued beyond his own lifetime. He symbolised his convictions by keeping in his bedroom a statue of Miguel de Cervantes' Don Quixote – an icon of honesty, conviction, perseverance and the continuous struggle against power and those who wield it. The symbolism was clearly understood and appreciated by his visitors over the years. Fathy also dedicated his life to an uncompromising battle to stop the widely prevalent forces of internationalism becoming the architectural expression of 'modern society'. He regarded internationalism as a forceful intrusion that obliterated meaning and social consciousness from architecture. He was aware that he was doomed not to win. But did he care? He persevered and left an enormous legacy. In time he radicalised his

Bimal Hasmukh Patel, Entrepreneurship Development Institute of India, Ahmedabad, India, 1987
Recipient of the Aga Khan Award for Architecture, 1992
Ahmedabad was founded in 1411 by Muslims, who endowed the city with a splendid collection of mosques, mausolea, courtyard houses, labyrinths of public thoroughfares and alleys, private cul-de-sacs and gates. Patel's design for the campus of the Entrepreneurship Development Institute of India was strongly influenced by his wish to establish a connection with this rich accumulation of India's past. The architect's organisational principles, as well as his use of a very limited palette of building materials – exposed brick, stone and wood, with a minimal application of reinforced concrete, steel trusses and corrugated aluminium sheet – directly reflect their traditional Islamic sources. The campus consists of residential facilities, classrooms, offices and a library, organised within seven buildings linked by two axes. An auditorium, to be built in the future, will complete the master plan.
The Aga Khan Award for Architecture commended Patel 'for his confident use of formal elements growing out of the Indo–Islamic architectural heritage'. A series of geometrically structured courtyards and loggias are the primary organising framework. The variation of open, closed and transitional spaces provides light and shade, and creates an inviting environment for work, interaction and repose.

Geoffrey Bawa, Chairman's Award

In 1979, Geoffrey Bawa was invited by President Jayewardene to design Sri Lanka's new parliament building at Kotte. At Bawa's suggestion, the swampy site was dredged to create an island at the centre of a vast artificial lake. Bawa's design for the parliament building appears to be an asymmetric composition of copper roofs floating above a series of terraces rising out of the water. Bawa incorporated abstract references to traditional Sri Lankan and South Indian architecture within a Modernist framework to create a powerful and yet serene architecture of continuity and progress.

One of Bawa's earliest projects, a courtyard house built in Colombo for Ena De Silva in 1961, was the first to fuse elements of traditional Sinhalese domestic architecture with modern concepts of open planning. The Bentota Beach Hotel of 1968, Sri Lanka's first purpose-built resort hotel, has a sense of place and continuity that has rarely been matched. During the early 1970s, Bawa developed ideas for the workplace in a tropical city, culminating in the State Mortgage Bank in Colombo, hailed at the time as one of the world's first bioclimatic high-rises. During the 1980s, he designed the new Ruhunu University near Matara, a matrix of pavilions and courtyards, arranged with careful casualness and a strong sense of theatre across a pair of rocky hills overlooking the southern ocean. This project enabled Bawa to demonstrate his mastery of external space and the integration of buildings in a landscape. A believer in the genius of place, he followed these ideas in three hotels built in Sri Lanka in the 1990s: the Kandalama, an austere jungle palace, snaking around a rocky outcrop on the edge of an ancient tank in the Dry Zone; the Lighthouse at Galle, defying the southern oceans from its boulder-strewn headland; and the Blue Water, a cool pleasure pavilion set within a sedate coconut grove on the edge of Colombo. All these structures demonstrate his genius for integrating architecture and landscape. His design in 1997 for the Jayawardene family's weekend retreat on the cliffs of Mirissa, is a phalanx of slender columns supporting a wafer-thin roof looking towards the southern ocean and the setting sun.

Two projects hold the key to an understanding of Bawa's work: the garden at Lunuganga that he has continued to fashion for almost 50 years, and his own house in Colombo's Bagatelle Road. Lunuganga is a distant retreat, an outpost on the edge of the known world, a civilised garden within the larger wilderness of Sri Lanka, transforming an ancient rubber estate into a series of outdoor rooms that evoke memories of Sacro Bosco and Stourhead. His own house, in contrast, is an introspective assemblage of courtyards, verandas and loggias, created by knocking together four tiny bungalows and adding a white entry tower that peers like a periscope across neighbouring rooftops towards the distant ocean. It is a haven of peace, an infinite garden of the mind, locked away within a busy and increasingly hostile city.

Throughout its long and colourful history, Sri Lanka has been subjected to strong outside influences from its Indian neighbours, Arab traders and European colonists, and has always succeeded in translating these elements into something new but intrinsically Sri Lankan. Bawa has continued this tradition. His architecture is a subtle blend of modernity and tradition, East and West, formal and picturesque. He has broken down the artificial segregation of inside and outside, building and landscape. He has drawn on tradition to create an architecture that is fitting to its place, and used his vast knowledge of the modern world to create an architecture that is of its time.

position and turned it into a battle against the totality of institutionalised architecture. I remember one day in 1972 when, after seeing a building with a curtain wall and mirrored glazing, he said: 'Look at the architect. He is so ashamed of his own design that he dares only to reflect the surrounding architecture.'

The intrinsic creativity, modesty and dedication of Fathy and his architecture have never been denied, even by his opponents. However, the failure of his solutions for the social forces in which he believed has been widely used as an argument against the traditionalist approaches of which he was a pioneer. Fathy's rural resettlement projects at New Gourna Village, Luxor (1953), and Bariz Village near Kharga (1964), were not successful because of social and economic realities – the villagers refused to settle in the new accommodation. The original inhabitants of Gourna, who based their living on clandestine archaeological digs on the grounds where their village had once stood, did not wish to move elsewhere for obvious reasons. This scarred Fathy's practice, which was based on communal participation. In fact, Fathy ingeniously remastered the traditional Nubian vaulting system of mud bricks without using any wooden formwork, instead corbelling the bricks to form vaults and domes. This simple construction technique yielded well-insulated, comfortable spaces and impressive

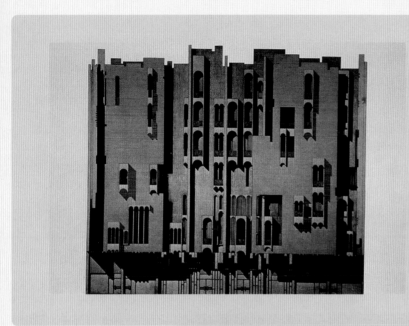

Lifetime Achievements of Rifat Chadirji, Chairman's Award
Rifat Chadirji, the Iraqi architect, critic and teacher, has
searched for an appropriate contemporary architectural
expression that synthesises elements of the rich Islamic
cultural heritage with key principles of the international
architecture of the 20th century. Chadirji believes that the
future of architecture lies in the lessons learned from its
past. His designs are transformations of regional forms
that seek to express, by means of abstraction, the
construction technologies used almost universally today,
while affirming the aesthetic values the latter engender.

His last assignment in Iraq was to serve as adviser to
the Municipality of Baghdad, then engaged in planning the
most extensive urban reconstruction in the history of the
city. Although the war between Iraq and Iran halted this
project, his vision of Baghdad's future townscape, in
conjunction with the rest of his life's work, still serves to
raise critical questions about the meanings of architecture
in Islamic society, and offers important examples for study.
His built work, projects, teaching and writings have helped
form a conscience and set goals for Arab and Muslim
architects everywhere.

Image: Federation of Industries, Baghdad, Iraq: etching of
main facade.

robust architectonics for architects and non-
architects to admire.

'Building with people', Fathy's principal tenet,
did not work at Bariz Village either. He was
therefore criticised not for his architecture but
for the negative reaction of the community.
In short, he was sadly undermined by those to
whom he dedicated his mission. Naturally this
was not a deliberate reaction against him by the
community. However, he was indirectly betrayed
by those whom he loved and wanted to help most.

Even though Fathy's priority was to help the
poor in order to improve their living conditions
through appropriate architecture, he ended up
building exquisite stone-masonry villas for the
well-off Cairo intelligentsia. Cynics who were
envious of his international reputation claimed

that he was 'writing about the poor and building for the
rich'. What they deliberately ignored was Fathy's belief
that if the leaders of Egyptian society appropriated
and made good use of his architecture for their high
aspirations and lifestyles, the underprivileged would
follow them. This dream did not materialise, at least
not in Fathy's lifetime.

The residence he shared with more than 30 much-
loved cats, a portion of an old Mamluk house next to
Saladin's Citadel on Darb el-Labbana, was frequented
by many who admired his goals and wished to benefit
from his wisdom. Those interested in talking to him, or
at least listening to what he professed, were offered an
open invitation to tea every afternoon. From 1960 all
the way through to the late 1980s, to have tea with
Fathy was an opportunity and a ritual not to be missed.
He was perhaps the only architect of international fame
for centuries with an open door for everyone. This
hospitality enabled him to form links with people all
over the world. That was how I met him for the first
time in 1969, and many times afterwards. He became
an undeclared guru for alternative architectural
discourse.

In the mission of cultural continuity, the design and
building of projects that respond to their historical,
natural and cultural contexts has been important.
Examples include the work of Iraqi architect Rifat
Chadirji, a pioneer in the realm of contextualism, and
Sri Lankan architect Geoffrey Bawa, an influential
proponent of an architecture that is environmentally
in harmony with tropical contexts; his great talent
in creating an architectural language that is fully
integrated with its site and place has been an
inspiration to the whole profession in the tropics.

Continuing in this tradition, there are many
architects who have generated a noble discourse that
has revealed the valour of simplicity, humility and a
sensitive understanding of the wider environment. The
development of creative techniques, building systems
and usage of materials has generated novel
architectural expressions in projects both minor and
major in scale. Their work also introduces new building
typologies for other architects to emulate.

German architect Frei Otto reinforced his
architectural commitment to tensile structures by
adapting them to the harsh climatic conditions of the
Arabian Peninsula. Danish architect Henning Larsen
developed novel Modern architectural expressions
by modernising courtyards and the circulation pattern
of souks. In a similar vein, US architect Louis Kahn
created an architectural solution based on the
northern Indian cultural heritage, which he
modernised with strong symbolism at the National
Assembly of Bangladesh in Dacca (1983), giving the
Islamic world one of its strongest architectural
expressions. French architect Jean Nouvel took the

For the last 25 years, the Aga Khan Award for Architecture has been exploring appropriate architecture for Muslims throughout the world. Thousands of people have contributed talent and intelligence to this endeavour to improve the built environment and, in so doing, to enrich the human condition.

idea of the lattice and the *mashrabiyya* (grilled wooden window screen) and reinterpreted it in terms of the most sophisticated building technology for the Arab World Institute in Paris (1987). Malaysian architect Ken Yeang has been providing solutions for bioclimatic high-rise buildings and proving that the high-rise and environmental concerns are not necessarily incompatible. Charles Correa derives his space configurations from the many expressions and uses of space developed in the multi-faith and multiethnic conditions of India. They should all be praised. They have been able to build in natural and urban environments while enhancing social and cultural values. Their large-scale buildings, approached with modesty and a keen understanding of culture and history, have yielded novel architectural expressions that have been acclaimed locally and internationally.

Last but never least, landscape projects that respond with creativity and sophistication in their use of natural forms and materials play a major role in projecting cultural identity in the context of open spaces. Parks offer relief from urban congestion and provide varied spaces for social interaction.

For the last 25 years, the Aga Khan Award for Architecture has been exploring appropriate architecture for Muslims throughout the world. Thousands of people have contributed talent and intelligence to this endeavour to improve the built environment and, in so doing, to enrich the human condition. In today's electronic age, people can share not only each other's hardships and misery but also their accomplishments and happiness. The responsible and responsive attitude of the Aga Khan Award for Architecture – to promote successful solutions to difficult problems in the built environment – remains as important today as it was a quarter of a century ago. However, there are many building types, problems and regions that have yet to be addressed. Good buildings for health, industry and housing, and schemes to repair both natural and man-made disasters, are all areas that the award must pursue with increasing rigour and determination. ⚼

Charles Correa, Vidhan Bhavan, Bhopal, India, 1996
Recipient of the Aga Khan Award for Architecture, 1998
Vidhan Bhavan, the new state assembly for the government of Madhya Pradesh, is located on a hill in the centre of Bhopal. Since the main access road is not axial but swings towards the site in an irregular pattern following the contours of the hill, the plan of the building and its interior gardens and courtyards was developed within an almost continuous circular exterior wall. This form established a visual unity and presence regardless of the direction from which one approaches it. The building's four main functions – a lower house, upper house, combined hall, and library – require extensive administrative facilities, meeting rooms, suites for the political leaders, cafeterias and common rooms. All of these diverse elements are linked by a series of gardens defined by two symmetrical architectural axes that intersect at the centre of the circle. These axes extend to the edges of the site and open into panoramic views of the surrounding city.

Vidhan Bhavan is conceived as a 'city within a city'. The use of local red stone, handmade ceramic tiles and painted surfaces refers to the architectural traditions of Madhya Pradesh: gateways, enclosures, courts, small domes and other architectural details that develop a new imagery based on traditional forms. Large contemporary murals, sculptures and paintings by local artists enliven the spaces. The jury commended the complex as 'the creation of an ensemble that provides a wide range of spatial experiences as one moves through the complex'.

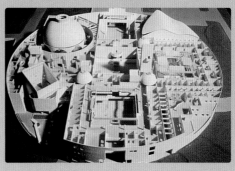

Community and Coherence

A senior adviser to the United Nations World Food Programme, **David B Roosevelt** has had a long career in senior management positions in philanthropic organisations. Through his direct work with various charitable organisations he has developed a strong regard for the cohesive power of community projects. Here he advocates a grass-roots approach to some of the problems that plague the Middle East and other nations in the Islamic world, building and progressing local communities where national infrastructures are insufficient or politically and economically bankrupt.

'Community' is a word with many meanings and connotations. It may be used broadly to describe humankind or society at large; or conversely to relate to a specific sector of the population, who share communal, religious, ethnic or other bonds of commonality. It may be demarcated by a geographic or regional limitation, or by a cultural or societal norm shared collectively. It is indeed a useful, if not misleading and often misunderstood, term used to relate to a collection of people drawn together for, or by, a common cause or good – call it collective ownership, perhaps – which provides the cohesion for existence and coexistence.

I say misleading and misunderstood because if one accepts that community implies a commonly accepted interest or ownership, then terms such as 'world community' or 'community of nations', in the broader sense of today, are a non sequitur. Before these lofty terms can have meaning, there must be existence of the more basic community – that deriving from the family or clan, a neighbourhood, village or town and, finally, a nation. Here, however, my thoughts and observations will relate largely to a notion of community created by common social and cultural mores, including religious beliefs, which bind the greater community of Islam.

I claim to be no expert, being neither a sociologist nor anthropologist. I am, though, like so many others living in our tumultuous world, an observant bystander, trying to deal with confusion and questioning, and airing concern for the rapid erosion of 'community' in our world. Much of my life has been spent in philanthropy, concentrating on building community at the most basic local level. This, in my view, is really what philanthropy is all about – providing a means, albeit limited and usually focused – to build cohesive community. Foundations, charities and NGOs, United Nations agencies, and even many corporate-giving programmes, are all ultimately dedicated to building cohesive communities, regardless of their programme focus or structural limitations. Some are enterprising and effective. Many, in my view, are woefully insular, lack direction and suffer a severe case of tunnel vision. But that is another topic for another day.

As one considers the community of the world's 1.2 billion Muslims, it is important to remember that we speak of lives scattered around the globe in a vast tapestry held together by the thread of Islam: 260 million Muslims live in the Arab world, the heartland of the community, but many more live in India (120 million), Pakistan, Bangladesh, Turkey, Southeast Asia, Europe, the US, Asia and Africa. The majority of the Islamic community today lives in electoral democracies, in countries that have considerable experience in democracy, and in countries where women have been elected prime ministers (India, Pakistan and Indonesia) well before such a thing occurred in most Western nations. Many Westerners use the words 'Islamic', 'Middle Eastern' and 'Arab' interchangeably, but this is wrong, for they do not mean the same thing, and I want to make some of these distinctions here. The 'Islamic community' is a broadly diverse and eclectic community of peoples living in all corners of the world, whose one voice of coherence is the respect and practice of Islam.

Today the Western world is much preoccupied with the Arab world or, more specifically, with the Middle East as but one part of the larger Islamic community. The Arabs share a great tradition as a civilisation with a long history of science, philosophy and military successes. They can be credited with the invention of algebra and

Barefoot Architects, Barefoot College, Tilonia, Rajasthan, 1988 and ongoing

Opposite, pages 34 & 36
This unique and very effective community scheme in India trains the rural semiliterate population to construct their own much-needed housing and rainwater-harvesting structures. See full description on p 37.

By the end of the Second World War and throughout the middle of the 20th century, the Arab world, newly independent from the shackles of the colonial powers of Europe, seemed poised to recapture all the glories of the past. Cities like Beirut, Damascus, Cairo and Baghdad were re-emerging as centres of culture, commerce and progressive advancement, whose citizens had an increasingly modern and secular attitude towards church and state.

the preservation of Aristotle when he had been forgotten in the West, and they have succeeded in wars against some of the great powers of the past. Islamic art and culture born in the Arab world were flourishing in sophistication as Europe languished in the Dark Ages. Indeed, it was the social and cultural strands of the Arab world that enabled it to survive many centuries of misrule and subjugation by wave after wave of conquerors.

By the end of the Second World War and throughout the middle of the 20th century, the Arab world, newly independent from the shackles of the colonial powers of Europe, seemed poised to recapture all the glories of the past. Cities like Beirut, Damascus, Cairo and Baghdad were re-emerging as centres of culture, commerce and progressive advancement, whose citizens had an increasingly modern and secular attitude towards church and state. Some of the days' leading educational and cultural institutions could be found in these centres of sophistication and enrichment, and the relationship between religions was, by and large, one of respect and mutuality, if not equanimity.

But something happened between then and now; a widening chasm of misunderstanding and suspicion opened between the Western and the Arab countries, and now we face the question of this article: How do we begin to heal the present to gain a better future, not solely through politics and trade, but through helping build communities and consensus between these two worlds?

In the 1950s pan-Arabism was flavoured with dreams of freedom, self-determination, unity and considerations of modernity. The whole region, perhaps for the first time in centuries, seemed to dream in one voice and with singular vision. Today, shockingly, almost every Arab country in the region can be said to be less free than 40 years ago. Problems such as local politics, poor choices in central planning, stagnating economies, dictatorships and repressive regimes have cracked and crumbled pan-Arabism.

In the 1950s, pan-Arabism was flavoured with dreams of freedom, self-determination, unity and considerations of modernity. The whole region, perhaps for the first time in centuries, seemed to dream in one voice and with singular vision. Today, shockingly, almost every Arab country in the region can be said to be less free than 40 years ago. Problems such as local politics, poor choices in central planning, stagnating economies, dictatorships and repressive regimes have cracked and crumbled pan-Arabism. Israel's wars against its Arab neighbours continue to deal blows and mark low points in the recent history of the region. Unlike Africa, where abject national poverty is often the rule rather than the exception, the problem in some parts of the Arab world, paradoxically, is not poverty but the oil wealth concentrated among its ruling and educated elite. This has acted as a disincentive to not only the growth and diversification of commercial enterprise, but also to the global conventions of fiscal transparency and accountability, which engagement with international markets require.

The very different tracks that the West and the Middle East have taken in the postwar period have been highlighted and exacerbated by the deep schism between the current US administration and the Middle East. Bush's mandate has been to export his administration's own form of 'democratic values' to the Middle East, without comprehending the results and implications of such a mandate, and the understandably adverse reactions from most Arab citizens.

How Can the Construction of Local Community Projects Help?
When governments fail or refuse to engage their people in constructive community-building, even across nations, the opportunity arises for the involvement of individual citizen action. When we think of community-building, or 'nation-building', we normally equate this as a function of government alone. In my view, the most successful architecture for building an effective civic society model is a collaborative effort between the people of a community who seize the opportunity to organise. This in itself is an expression of democratic self-determination. In the end, as has been observed, the most successful and ultimately effective forms of political action are those which emanate at the local level.

The building of strong community is a bottom-up, rather than a top-down, process. It relies on the empowerment and engagement of individual citizen action rather than sole dependence on public authorities. People, not governments, build community, although where a strong public/private partnership exists and collaboration between all sectors is encouraged, the process is tremendously enhanced.

In the Islamic world, and through the teachings of the Koran, there is a heritage of charity and, by extension, philanthropic enterprise; of the desire and will to promote the welfare of others through voluntary giving. It is within this tradition, I believe, that organised philanthropy can play an extremely important role in the building and rebuilding of community in the Islamic world and the Middle East; a potentially powerful resource for bringing together the vast diversity of local and regional interests.

There exist today several philanthropic foundations throughout the world whose activities either directly or indirectly provide programmatic and/or financial resources for the community-building process. One striking example of philanthropy at work in some Muslim countries is the Aga Khan Foundation. It is 'a modern vehicle for traditional philanthropy in the Ismaili Muslim community', whose mission is 'to develop and promote creative solutions to problems that impede social development'. Yet further examples are the Open Society Institute and the Soros Foundations Network, with operations in more than 50 countries including Turkey, Iran, Iraq, Jordan, Israel, Bahrain, Lebanon and Egypt. The Soros Foundations' activities in many of the post-communist countries of eastern Europe, particularly as a resource for democratic community empowerment and enablement, are well known. And of course the work of the Ford Foundation, with its wide assortment of programmes in, particularly, developing nations, is also worthy of note.

But as noteworthy as these and so many other foundations are in contributing to community-building activities in numerous areas of the world, there is another philanthropic model that I think could well serve some of the Islamic and Middle Eastern societies. This is the concept of a 'community-based' foundation, which in recent years has proven extremely adaptable in other emerging nations. It is a flexible and effective means for involving citizens in an effort to structurally improve their own communities. In many ways, the concept epitomises the Islamic tradition of individual and collective self-help as a focal point of reference for defining that most important element of 'community' – the sense of personal identity and cohesion of belonging.

A community foundation might best be described as a foundation run by members of the community, for the benefit of the community, in order to fit a niche for addressing unfulfilled needs. Although generally defined by specific geographic reference, it brings together a much broader participation of individuals from across cultural, social and religious boundaries within a structured framework, to encourage investment in the community-building process. The vision of a community foundation is underpinned by its dexterity and flexibility in addressing the problems and issues of a community. It has the ability to adapt itself to diverse local characteristics, even to opposing views, by structuring and sponsoring programmes that emphasise cohesion within its outreach.

As observed in a study published by the Transatlantic Community Foundation Network, 'community foundation[s are] being organized in the most unlikely places because individuals ... realize that while we are inextricably tied to one another around the world, it is in localities that problems must be addressed. Globalization promises that we are connected in many new ways, but it is increasingly apparent that problems must be addressed and opportunities seized, first in communities and geographic spaces close to us.' This study further concludes that: 'Those elements of social solidarity [have] been longstanding manifestations of

Programmatically, a community foundation can, and should, be as diverse as the people it aims to represent. The more 'general purpose' its programme areas, the more flexibility it has in addressing the spectrum of community issues and concerns.

strong societies in China, Africa, South America, and many other places [and I would include the Arab and Middle Eastern Islamic communities] where the recognition of mutual obligation [has built] a powerful civic fabric.'

In practical terms, community foundations share several characteristics that make them unique and distinct from other philanthropic and governmental endeavours. Specifically, they tend to be autonomous entities, operated for charitable rather than profit motives and independent of control or influence from other organisations or government. They are geographically focused, thus concentrating on the specific needs of a particular community, of which they become very knowledgeable with in-depth understanding of the opportunities, issues and people. By its very definition, a community foundation is inclusive, involving all types of citizens, their interests, visions and cultural characteristics. Its governance will include a cross section of the entire population to ensure that the collective interests of the people are voiced and represented. It can also be an important vehicle for introducing innovation as it explores new ideas and approaches in working with the community at large as well as other institutional resources. But one of its most important attributes is the ability and willingness to be transparent and accountable in its policies and practices.

Programmatically, a community foundation can, and should, be as diverse as the people

it aims to represent. The more 'general purpose' its programme areas, the more flexibility it has in addressing the spectrum of community issues and concerns. Programmes could include everything from the building of school facilities, expansion and improvement of educational content, provision of playing fields or housing for the elderly, support of the arts and cultural expression, the environment, architectural rehabilitation. In other words, it can be responsive to an almost never-ending array of issues and needs.

Some of the newer community foundations can be found in countries just emerging with fledgling democracies, such as in the former communist bloc nations, including Russia. These countries have found this model to be particularly effective in developing the sense of citizen responsibility so necessary to the building of civil society. For the first time, direct citizen participation is encouraged at the local level, thus engaging individuals in recognition of their rights and duties as citizens within their society.

Another important long-term benefit of adaptation of the community foundation concept is its power to instil a sense of permanent community philanthropy. To this end, many foundations have been successful, after demonstrating their value and trustworthiness, in building a base of permanent assets that ensure a continuity of purpose and programmes in the future. All the work of a community foundation can be seen as an investment for both the present and the future, to enrich and build coherence between all sectors of the community. It fosters partnerships and collaboration where previously none existed, providing a focal point for discussion and resolution of often opposing ideals. As a community-based institution, the foundation transfers the decision-making ability from government bureaucracy to citizen self-determination.

Although there are no definitive solutions to building community and coherence in the Middle East, it is my opinion that reliance on government-imposed solutions alone, and in particular those imposed by foreign influences, will be ineffective for the citizens of this region. It is important that solutions flow from local communities themselves, to regenerate and enrich the cultural heritage of the Middle East. It may seem simplistic, but when given the opportunity to participate in their own self-determination, people become empowered to solve their own problems.

Barefoot Architects
Barefoot Architects
Barefoot Architects
Barefoot Architects

Barefoot Architects, Barefoot College, Tilonia, Rajasthan, India, 1988 and ongoing

'Never Let School Interfere with your Education.'
— Mark Twain

Barefoot College is the only college in India built by the poor, for the poor. Between 1986 and 1988, men and women from poor communities were consulted on how they would like to construct a college of their own. How it was possible to use traditional knowledge, local materials, village skills and demonstrate, in the process, how relevant and important their practical wisdom was to preserving and conserving the architectural skills fast dying or, indeed, disappearing from traditional communities at large.

Barefoot College was founded in 1972 as the Social Work and Research Centre (SWRC); its founder Bunker Roy believed it was possible to train barely literate and unemployed rural men and women from remote villages to be 'barefoot' water and solar engineers, teachers, doctors, communicators and architects. The idea was that they develop self-respect and self-esteem by serving their own communities and, as a result, prevent mass migration to the cities.

The community of users – male and female engineers, hand-pump mechanics, traditional puppeteers, village masons, midwives, night-school teachers – all sat down and contributed to the ideas that went into the concept, as well as to the building of the college. They felt strongly that if they had to live and work in the college they had every right to design, shape and build it together. An illiterate farmer with 12 other Barefoot architects (semiliterate though not uneducated!) drew plans on the ground of how they would like the college to look. The layout was eventually prepared by a young architect barely out of architectural school, who was asked to make a blueprint, a basic requirement for the government funding the college was seeking.

The Barefoot Architects insisted that the buildings face the wind, so that the natural circulation within the courtyards would keep them cool. The women wanted a place to cook in the open courtyard, and used traditional knowledge and materials for waterproofing the roofs of the campus which, to this day, have never leaked! With great foresight, the Barefoot Architects connected the roofs of all the buildings to collect rainwater in a 400,000-litre underground tank, and over this built a stage for 5,000 people to sit and watch performances of puppeteers or street theatre. This was quite remarkable in the late 1980s, when even many professional architects remained ignorant of the importance of collecting rainwater as part of their basic designs. A semiliterate Muslim blacksmith fabricated the door and window frames, as well as solar cookers and heaters.

Barefoot is the only college in India which derives all of its power from the sun. Over 40 kilowatts of solar panels provide power for the 20 computers, the photocopying machines, electronic mail, audiovisual equipment, and 500 lights and fans for the whole campus. The panel installation was carried out by Barefoot solar engineers, headed by an Indian priest who still looks after a Hindu temple and has carried out 10 years of rural schooling.

Since the early 1990s, the Barefoot Architects have constructed 200 low-cost dwellings for the homeless and over 450 rooftop rainwater-harvesting structures in schools, collecting 33 million litres – when it rains! As a result, the attendance of girls at these schools has increased because previously only drinking water was available.

The ideas have helped lift the marginalised communities out of poverty and given them tremendous hope. By bringing community knowledge and skills into mainstream thinking in modern technology, engineering and architecture, Barefoot College has demonstrated the relevance of development that is community owned and community managed, and what we mean by sustainability. As the late President Neyerre said: 'People cannot be developed. They develop themselves.' ⌂

— Bunker Roy, Barefoot Architects of Tilonia

Gropius and Fathy Remembered

As a member of the Policy Planning Council of the US Department of State from 1961 to 1965, during the Kennedy and Johnson administrations, **William R Polk** was in charge of American planning for much of the Islamic world. Here he describes how as a Harvard academic, leading up to that period, he accompanied Walter Gropius to Baghdad and encountered Hassan Fathy in Egypt.

Although not an architect, I have been privileged to know a wide range of leaders in the field. Even better, watching them at work and discussing their ideas, I was able to see their reactions to the challenges they faced in trying encapsulate the aims and desires of those for whom they designed their projects. Here, I would like to single out two of them who, for me, were particularly interesting.

Walter Gropius was nearing the end of his long and varied career when I met him. He had just retired as dean of the school of architecture at Harvard, and was the *primus inter pares* of The Architects Collaborative (TAC) in Cambridge, Massachusetts. His firm had been awarded a contract to design a new university in Baghdad, but the 1958 coup d'état caused the cancellation of the project.

As it happened, I had just returned from Baghdad where, a few years earlier, I had been a fellow of the Rockefeller Foundation. As I was studying Iraqi politics, I was familiar with all of the civilians who had overthrown the monarchy, and wrote two articles for the *Atlantic* on the aspirations of the new government. Gropius read my pieces and invited me to come for a chat. The meeting turned out to be the start of a long and delightful friendship.

Soon afterwards we went to Baghdad together, where we resurrected and, indeed, greatly enlarged the university design contract. This represented the positive aspect of our mission; the negative aspect was that the government, under a different leadership, exhibited some of the ugly features that would mark the later regime of Saddam Hussein. These characteristics horrified 'Grope' (as his American friends affectionately knew him). They reminded him of his time in Germany in the early 1930s when megalomania was state policy. And, so reminded, he poured forth a stream of his memories of those times during the days we sat holed up in a hotel awaiting the final stage of our negotiations.

The final stage was profoundly disturbing to him but was, I admit, profoundly amusing to me. When everything had been agreed 'at the working level', we were summoned to the office of the then 'sole leader', Prime Minister Abdul Karim Qasim,[1] for what we had been told would be the signing of the contract. I warned Grope that he should expect trouble. It came quickly.

As we took our seats at the cabinet table, klieg lights blazed forth and television cameras began to whirl. We were being informed, not so subtly, that the prestige of the prime minister was on exhibit before the entire nation.

Qasim began with a short statement complimenting Gropius on his preliminary work, but at the same time stating that the agreed fee was far too high: the Iraqi people demanded that it be scaled down.

Gropius turned to me, dismayed, and whispered: 'What shall I do?' I suggested that as a gesture of goodwill – since in fact the fee was really more than any of us had expected – he offer to reduce it by half a per cent. He nodded and asked me to translate this to Qasim, at which point Qasim waived the concession aside, saying: 'I do not deal in half percentages.'

I relayed this to Gropius, who sighed: 'You do whatever you think best.' His (and my) worry was that whatever concession was made, it, too, would be regarded as insufficient. Once on that slippery slope, we would find no firm ground.

> By this time I had guessed that the television cameras making such a clatter in the room were, in fact, empty. They were just a prop for the bargaining. So I smiled and said that I fully understood the prime minister's position. Half percentages were clearly not worth his time. What was important to the Iraqi people was that the magnificent new project go ahead rapidly to meet the needs and desires of their youth. So, I suggested, let us just get on with the job at the agreed fee.

By this time I had guessed that the television cameras making such a clatter in the room were, in fact, empty. They were just a prop for the bargaining. So I smiled and said that I fully understood the prime minister's position. Half percentages were clearly not worth his time. What was important to the Iraqi people was that the magnificent new project go ahead rapidly to meet the needs and desires of their youth. So, I suggested, let us just get on with the job at the agreed fee.

Qasim appeared startled, turned and glared at the Iraqi officials with whom we had negotiated, and then looked at me and burst out laughing. I too laughed. Although he didn't know what had happened, Gropius nervously joined in. Qasim then gestured to the cameramen to stop the clatter and douse the lights.

> In the earliest mosques, and in many of the larger modern buildings, the space is not covered. However, for the Baghdad University project, Gropius designed a stunningly beautiful dome, cast in concrete and flying almost like a tent, with the supporting corners set in pools of water to reflect inward on the ceiling.

This done, he pointed his finger at me and said: 'You really must make a concession.'

'Yes, your excellency,' I said, 'you are right – let's agree on one per cent.'

'Done,' he replied, and we all shook hands. Somewhat bewildered, Gropius whispered to me: 'Did you agree that we would do it ... free?'

With this essential first step out of the way, Gropius turned his attention to the really important tasks. One that particularly engaged him was what would become the centrepiece of the new campus – the mosque.

What, really, was a mosque? We discussed this almost endlessly, and Grope poured over books of illustrations of what had been built under the Mamluk regime in the early Middle Ages in Egypt, under the Umayyads and others in Islamic Spain (al-Andalus), in Safavid Iran, Mogul India and Ottoman Turkey. He found, of course, enormous variety in detail, but finally convinced himself that, in essence (the essence being something that, as an architect, it seems to me he was always seeking) a mosque was really very simple: it was composed of three elements.

The first element is what is known in Arabic as the mihrab. A mihrab can exist independent of any building. To pray, Bedouin customarily draw a line in the sand with a half circle in the middle pointing towards Mecca. For them, this plot of land is an ephemeral mosque. When incorporated within a building, the mihrab is, for the Muslim architect, the heart of the place of worship but, for the non-Muslim architect, it is of minor importance to the design. It does, however, have a fascinating history.

The tradition from which the mihrab derives is ancient, and probably comes from the ancient Egyptian 'door of heaven', through Sassassian palace throne rooms to later Christian niches. It is surely one of the most enduring and important of architectural forms, although one that is physically not particularly impressive. I think it is fair to say that it did not much interest Gropius.

The second, and to Gropius, the most important element, was what we call a minaret. The word minaret comes from *manarah* which, like most Arabic words, has multiple meanings – candlestick, lighthouse, signpost and watchtower. The earliest mosques did not have minarets. Tradition holds that the first man to summon worshippers to prayer (Arabic: *muazzin*) just climbed up on to a roof. But, from the building of the first great mosque in Qairawan, when Islam was less than a century old, minarets became a standard feature. Like the bell tower of a church, the minaret also came to be, over the centuries, the very symbol of the place of worship. For Gropius it was the key element of the mosque.

The third element was the space in which worshippers would assemble. In the earliest mosques, and in many of the larger modern buildings, the space is not covered. However, for the Baghdad University project, Gropius designed a stunningly beautiful dome, cast in concrete and flying almost like a tent, with the supporting corners set in pools of water to reflect inward on the ceiling. This piece of the university was actually built as planned, but, alas, as I saw during my visits to Baghdad before the American incursion in February 2003, it is already cracked, peeling and fading. Although, in my opinion, it is one of the most beautiful mosques, it is, like one of the great ziggurats of ancient Mesopotamia, subsiding into a ruin. I am glad Grope is not alive to see it today.

It is difficult to conjure up a figure more different from Walter Gropius than is Hassan Fathy. In a curious way, I suppose, I was the link between them. Not only did I introduce them, but I tried, though not very successfully, to make each appreciate the art of the other.

I first met Hassan in 1954 when, on behalf of the Ford Foundation, I was editing a supplement to a magazine entitled *Perspective of the Arab World*. My task was to illustrate contemporary trends in the Arab countries, a task which took me all over the area trying to identify interesting, but then little-known, people in the arts. I found Hassan almost by accident. Although several mutual friends had suggested his name, we actually met when I visited the apartment I had lived in, in an old Mamluk palace, years before. Hassan was now living there. He invited me in for tea.

A born teacher, Hassan had one consuming passion – to recapture architecture from the architects, to give it back to the people. In his Egypt, that meant enabling poor people to build their dwellings more or less as the

Right and following spread
'We need a system that allows the traditional way of cooperation to work in our society. We must subject technology and science to the economy of the poor and penniless. We must add the aesthetic factor because the cheaper we build the more beauty we should add to respect man.'
— Hassan Fathy

Hassan Fathy, an Egyptian architect, artist and poet, wanted to understand what the pre-industrial buildings of Egypt had to teach us about climate control and economical construction techniques, and to find ways of putting them to contemporary use. The splendid urban housing forms of Cairo, ingeniously shaded and ventilated by means of their two-storey halls, *mashrabiyyas* (intricate timber screens applied externally to windows) and courtyards, were not replicable because the building traditions that produced them had disappeared. They were to become an inspiration for Fathy's later work. But the rural areas abounded in ancient mud-brick forms, and were still being produced by rural masons. These houses consisted of inclined arches and vaults, built without shuttering, domes on squinches built over square rooms in a continuing spiral, semi-domed alcoves and other related forms. Fathy wanted Egypt's rural poor to learn, once again, to build shelters for themselves.

Fathy created more than 30 projects and several villages, most of which were partially or completely realised. His book *Architecture for the Poor* brought his work to international attention; it described his experience in planning and building the village of New Gourna, using mud bricks and employing traditional Egyptian architectural features such as enclosed courtyards and domed and vaulted roofing. Relocating an entrenched community of amateur rural archaeologists, making a tidy living from their habitations over the royal necropolis in Luxor, offered Hassan Fathy an opportunity to create a viable solution to the rural housing problem in Egypt. But instead of using a limited number of unit types, Fathy decided to design individual houses to meet the individual needs of each family. In fairness to Mr Fathy, if his brave project at New Gourna failed, it did not do so entirely because of his singular approach to programming and form. The villagers, for obvious reasons, were not overexcited about being relocated to New Gourna.

In 1980 Hassan Fathy received the Aga Khan Award for Architecture, and the Gold Medal of the Union of International Architects in 1984.
— Sabiha Foster

ancient Egyptians had done, with the mud of the Nile. 'His' Egyptians had forgotten how, and those who guided them had adopted both Western designs and Western materials.

Would I like to go with him to a village he was helping to build to see what his 'alternative' architecture meant? Of course I would.

So we went up river to 'New' Gourna near the great archaeological site of Luxor. Interspersed with tea and cookies (Hassan's weakness) and bouts of listening to scratchy recordings of Bach on a hand-cranked record player, he laid out for me his philosophy of architecture.

His was a philosophy constrained by the harsh realities of life, for the vast majority of contemporary Egyptians lived at subsistence level. Statisticians thought of them as earning far less than a dollar a day, but the reality was that they earned virtually no money at all. It wasn't just that modern building materials, cement and steel, and even wood which had to be imported, were a drain on the country's 'hard' currency, but that almost anything that required even 'soft' currency was beyond their reach.

Egypt was not alone in this harsh reality. A newly completed study for the World Bank showed that at least a billion people in the developing world would

die early and live stunted lives because of unsanitary, uneconomic and ugly housing. And this was the case not only in developing countries: America was beginning to realise the terrible costs of its slums. But America had an option: it could spend large amounts of money, as it soon was to do in its 'urban renewal' programme to upgrade housing. Egypt did not have that option.

What really differentiated Hassan from others, I believe, was that he embraced this reality as an opportunity. He began with a simple fact: like all animals, human beings always managed to create some form of shelter for themselves. The art of the architect was to help them do a better job of it. He approached this task in three ways: design, labour and materials.

For materials, there was little choice. Wood was unobtainable. Since before the First Dynasty, Egypt had to import what it could not do without. Wood was a great luxury, and the beautiful arabesque-panelled doors we see in Egyptian museums were made of scraps that a Western carpenter would have thrown away. For the peasant house-builder, wooden beams were beyond luxury. Steel was even more precious. Whatever Egypt produced went into the modern economy. Even the peasant who had an iron tip on his plough was a rich man. And concrete, although increasingly produced in Egypt, was expensive and, at the time, still scarce.

Concrete was Hassan's pet hate. He liked to quote statistics proving that it was not only expensive but inefficient; it offered little protection from the intense heat of the Egyptian summer, and houses built of it, he scoffed, were more ovens than homes. Only mud was left.

Hassan's colleagues and responsible government officials were dismissive: he was backward, not modern, and, worse, he was treating the people as little better than animals. Concrete was modern; mud was humiliating. Worse, it would collapse.

Hassan countered by arranging tours of ancient Egyptian sites where mud-brick structures were still standing after several thousand years, and by demonstrating that mud brick was a much better insulator than concrete. As we sat in the living room he had built for himself in 'his' village, New Gourna, I believed him. The room was pleasantly cool despite the fierce outside heat.

Best of all, he argued, mud was right under the peasant's feet. He didn't have to buy it. He just had to dig it up as he always had (to make irrigation ditches and ponds in which he raised fish and kept ducks), shape it into bricks, leave them in the sun to dry and stack them up.

Stacking them up as walls was simple; what was difficult was making roofs. The ancients had found a way to do it without supporting beams, but their technique had been forgotten. Resurrecting and refining it was the architect's task.

The trick was a dome. Against a mud plaster parabola as guide, a man could stack bricks in a way that each supported the next. Best of all, he could be taught this method in a few hours. Then, by leaving a small hole in the top of the resulting dome, perhaps capped with a piece of black metal, warm air would be sucked out and replaced by cooler air from ground level. As I had found in Hassan's room, it worked.

Pinpointing the cost of such work was difficult, but Hassan estimated that with the few things the peasant could not supply, such as water pipes and sanitary fittings, his typical house would cost about 15 per cent of the cheapest contract-built housing in Egypt.

Hassan's houses were not just affordable and comfortable; they were beautiful. Technique and materials lent themselves to moulded, plastic, flowing forms. New Gourna was a delight to the eye.

But it all failed. Hassan never wavered in his belief, and has since become something of a cult figure, but, not unlike Gropius, he died an unfulfilled artist. Each was, in his different way, defeated by human nature. Few of Gropius's grand ideas were realised and his most famous housing project, it must be admitted, displays a certain disdain for those who would live in it, who quickly did what they could to alter it in ways he found ugly. Hassan, to the contrary, was profoundly respectful, but respectful of an idealised people. The people of Old Gourna were not ideal, and they did not want to move to his ideal village. They did not care that New Gourna was beautiful. What they cared about was that Old Gourna lay atop an archaeological site whose tombs they robbed for saleable treasures. Old Gourna was not only their home but their livelihood. So Hassan's Gourna, like Gropius's mosque, is today a ruin.

Failure or unfulfilled vision that these experiments may have been, I look back upon the lives of these two friends, these two noble men, with a certain sadness, but with gratitude for the visions they shared with me.

Note
1 Abdul Karim Qasim was an army officer who, like many Iraqis, disliked the socially conservative and pro-Western policies of the monarchy. He overthrew the Iraqi monarchy in 1958 and became head of the newly formed Republic of Iraq. This movement was widely supported by the people and is still referred to as the revolution of the 14 July. He was a popular leader who tried to steer Iraq through an era when pro-Arab nationalism was at its peak in the Arab world. He began genuine attempts to develop the country and to improve its infrastructure, but on 8 February 1963 officers of the Baath Party overthrew his government and killed Qasim after a phony trial.

Background Note

The architectural backdrop to William Polk's essay is a fascinating one. In his capacity as adviser to the mayor of Baghdad, the Iraqi architect Rifat Chadirji was instrumental in commissioning international architects to build large-scale complexes in the city. Though Polk doesn't say so, one imagines Chadirji's interest in Gropius's use of screen-wall systems, which used a structural steel frame to support the floors and allowed the external glass walls to continue without interruption. We can only guess at conversations about Gropius's use of technology as a basis for transforming building into a science of precise mathematical calculations.

Be that as it may, some of the largest commissions in Iraq were given to The Architects Collaborative (TAC), an American design team founded by Gropius in 1945 whilst a professor at Harvard. Gropius's advocacy of industrialised building was synonymous with teamwork and an acceptance of standardisation and prefabrication. TAC embodied this belief in the value of teamwork, and came to be admired for its extensive range of projects, which included public and private school buildings and hospitals in Massachusetts.

The architects Chadirji involved in the Baghdad project were Frank Lloyd Wright (opera house), Le Corbusier (sports hall), Walter Gropius (university city), Alvar Aalto (art museum), Werner March (museum) and Pier Luigi Nervi. Of these, only the sports hall and the university city were completed (in 1960).

Gropius designed the university city in collaboration with the Iraqi architect Hisham A Munir. Its original 1957 plan was for a vast complex of buildings, to be constructed in an extensive area of open and enclosed spaces. Planned by the Ministry of Housing and Works in Baghdad, it was scheduled in three phases: the first to accommodate 5,000 students, the second 8,000 students, and the final phase a total of 12,000 students. The main auditorium has a seating capacity for 18,000. Designed as a small city, the campus consists of three faculties: engineering, science and the humanities. Surrounding the central plaza is the academic nucleus, where the buildings stand close together in order to create areas of shadow necessary for the very hot climate. The windows generally face north and south, and for cooling purposes some of the roofs and walls were transformed into water walls by the German sculptor Norbert Kricke.

It's worth mentioning that Iraq has produced a number of interesting architects and two major contemporary figures – Mohamed Saleh Makiya and Rifat Chadirji. Like Makiya, Chadirji maintained that local traditions were a determining element of 'continuous architecture'. His life has been devoted to the central issue of our times: How do we reconcile the cultural and social traditions of a country with the realities of rapid technological change and a growing internationalism in the arts? If Makiya did not accept that technology should dominate architecture, Chadirji attempted to integrate his interpretation of regional traditions into contemporary developments.

Chadirji's work embraces an extensive range of building types, from commercial, educational and residential to those dedicated to social welfare, in which are manifested the new challenges of more socially responsible architectural commissions. It includes housing complexes in Kuwait (1967–8), a cinema and office building in Bahrain (1968), plans for a hospital in Riyadh (1977), for the Dharan Medical Centre and Dental Clinic (1977), and for the National Theatre in Abu Dhabi (1977). Since 1983, Chadirji has lived in Europe, devoting himself to research. The most significant aspect of his work is his insight into the process of creating an architecture that merges ancient and modern into a new solution.

Projects continue to be given mainly to foreign architectural firms; commissions for residential architecture in various sectors of Baghdad have focused on integrating traditional elements into contemporary urban requirements. The result is a variety of building types that explore regional identity, some more successfully than others. One such example is the National Bank, a high-rise concrete structure dominated by a large interior courtyard, designed in 1966 by Arne Jacobsen and built after his death by his successors Dissing & Weitling.

In 1956, Hisham A Munir began planning and building the second largest university in Iraq – the University of Mosul. Mosul shows an assimilation of traditional elements, especially in the contemporary use of domed structures in the central library and the mosque. Munir's collaboration with TAC produced the Sheraton hotels in Baghdad and Basra (1981), though the latter was largely destroyed in the Iran–Iraq war. Other commissions include the Iraqi Reinsurance Company (1976) and Agricultural Complex (1975) in Baghdad, and the Al-Sabah Complex in Kuwait (1976).

TAC went out of business in 1995 due to political problems in the Middle East. ∞

— Sabiha Foster

Geometry and the House of Worship

'The Lotus Temple is a hymn to that ephemeral world where art and science enmesh with the architecture of Life.' **Sabiha Foster** describes this Baha'i House of Worship, in New Delhi, which was completed in 1986 by Fariborz Sahba.

In the 12th-century Seljuk Mescid-i Melik in Kerman,[1] Iran, a mihrab features a lotus flower. However, ornamental use of the lotus dates back well before the 12th century. In 3100 BC, the lotus was the emblem of Upper Egypt, and temple pillars from this period often have lotus-carved capitals. In a bas-relief in King Darius's 518 BC capital city of Persepolis, the king and his court are shown holding lotus flowers. And the lotus ornament also abounds in Assyriac,[2] Syrian and Carthaginian temple friezes and capitals.

The lotus has been a unifying symbol in many cultures and religions from the Egyptian and early Vedic to Buddhism, Christianity and Islam. Hindu writings say that, at the sound of the first Om, the primordial ocean brought forth 'a wondrous golden lotus, resplendent as the sun, which floated upon the lonely waters'. From Om issued the trinity of Brahma, Vishnu and Siva – all seated on golden lotuses.

In Mahayana Buddhism, the lotus symbolises creation and regeneration, the state of the initiate and, ultimately, of all beings, who will be reborn on lotus flowers. The colour of the lotus also has meaning: the white lotus is the symbol of spiritual perfection and enlightenment; the red lotus signifies the original nature and purity of the heart; blue symbolises the triumph of the spirit over the senses; and the pink lotus is associated with the Buddha himself. The *padmasana*, the lotus throne, is the symbol of the *dvija*, or twice-born, Shakyamuni Buddha, and represents the mastery of the spirit over the material world.

Perhaps the most poetic use of the lotus is in the Indian myth, which says that Brahma sat on a lotus blossom and dreamt the universe into being. In mystical Buddhism this is interpreted to mean the spiritually unconscious heart that blossoms when consciousness is awakened. In Buddhism, the lotus also symbolises the simultaneous nature of causality, as it produces both flowers and seeds at the same time. In this interpretation, the nine worlds[3] correspond to 'cause', and enlightenment to 'effect'. Both exist simultaneously within us, which is why Buddhist teachings say that the chanting of the Lotus Sutra causes the state of enlightenment, or Buddhahood,[4] to emerge within us.

Described as 'cosmic humanism', meaning unitive consciousness, the Lotus Sutra is an ancient banner of unity. It teaches that the inner determination of one individual can transform everything. Our ordinary perception leads us to believe that we need to perform an action to receive its effect. However, Buddhist teaching reveals that this future effect is already inherent within the act itself. The implication here is that our future is being shaped by our present actions. It is a teaching that gives ultimate expression to the infinite potential inherent in the life of every human being.

Memorable buildings have been created throughout history by Mesopotamian, Egyptian, Indian, Islamic and Christian architects who understood the mathematics of perpetual motion and synergy – what Buckminster Fuller called 'the fourth dimension'.

Fariborz Sahba was asked to design a house of worship that would honour the splendid spiritual and cultural heritage of India, and be synonymous with the cardinal principle of Baha'i teachings – the unity of religions: 'The gift of God to this enlightened age is the knowledge of the Oneness of religion.'[5]

Neither Buddhism nor the Baha'i faith started out as separatist movements, but as unifying movements of their original faiths. Both became religions in their own right only after resistance from theological orthodoxy.

Baha-ullah taught that there is one God, who progressively reveals his will to humanity, and that each of the great religions brought by the messengers[6] of God – Moses, Krishna, Buddha, Zoroaster, Jesus and Mohammed – represents a successive stage in the spiritual development of civilisation. Baha-ullah taught that throughout history, these successive revelations have been the chief civilising force. The agents of this process have been perceived as the founders of separate religious systems, but their common purpose has always been to bring humanity to spiritual and moral maturity. The Baha'is honour Baha-ullah as the most recent in this line of messengers, who brought teachings that address the moral and spiritual challenges of the modern world.

Om mani padme hum. The life of all is but a dewdrop, 'a jewel at the heart of the lotus'.

The growth of the lotus plant symbolises the evolution of the soul from the sludge of materialism, through the waters of experience, into the light of Being. Of all the water plants, only the lotus, because of the strength of its stem, rises above the surface of the water and bears buds, blossoms and seed pods all at the same time. This has come to signify the timelessness of Time – the past, present and future as a continuum. Its most remarkable particularity is that the lotus seed has within it a perfectly formed embryo plant, which symbolises the enfoldment of the inner, divine potential. It also suggests two parallels: the first between the spiritual and physical planes, and the second between cosmic creation and spiritual rebirth.

'The very diversity of the human race is, in fact, a means for creating a world based on unity rather than uniformity. It is not by the suppression of differences that we will arrive at unity, but rather by an increased awareness of and respect for the intrinsic value of each separate culture, and indeed, of each individual. It is not diversity itself which is the cause of conflict, but rather our immature attitude towards it, our intolerance and misconceptions of others.'[7]

The Lotus Temple (completed in 1986), took six years to construct, and sits in a 26-acre park in Delhi. The complex, lotus-shaped superstructure houses the auditorium area and a basement (which contains the electrical and plumbing components). Nine pools of water surround the building, connecting to it via walkways, balustrades, stairs and bridges. An ancillary block contains the reception area, library, administrative block and public facilities. This building is a tribute to human inspiration, ingenuity and computer technology. It is the world's largest poured-in-place concrete structure.

Each component of the temple is repeated nine times. Seen from the outside, there are three sets of petals made from concrete shells and clad in white marble panels, fixed to the concrete surface with specially designed stainless-steel anchors and brackets. Ten thousand square metres of marble was used, and each panel was cut to the required size and shape before being transported to site. The outermost set of nine petals opens outwards and forms the nine entrances around the annular hall. The next set of nine petals points inwards. The third set appears to be partially closed, rising above the rest, and houses the main structure of the central hall. Nine radial beams near the top provide lateral support. The lotus is open at the top where, at the level of the radial beams, a glass-and-steel roof provides protection from rain and facilitates the entrance of light into the auditorium. Below the entrance and outer petals, nine massive arches rise in a ring, and nine entrances lead into the main auditorium. Lateral movement, created by temperature changes and wind, is provided for by a neoprene pad, which rests between the radial ribs and the top of the interior dome.

The building uses natural ventilation. Summers are hot in Delhi, and humidity, though high, varies. The constant draughts of cool air passing over the nine surrounding pools of water flow into the auditorium and out through the top. Openings at the base and at the top draw in warm air from the hall and expel it through the top of the dome. The ventilation is complemented by two sets of fans arranged in the dome to cool the concrete shells and prevent transference of heat into the auditorium, and to funnel air from the auditorium into the cool basement, from where it is recycled back into the auditorium.

The Lotus Temple has about 4 million visitors a year, making it the most visited building in the world.

The entire superstructure functions as a skylight. The interior dome is spherical and patterned after the inner folds of the lotus blossom. Light filters through these folds and is diffused throughout the auditorium. The central bud consists of 27 petals, and is held by nine open petals, each of which functions like a skylight. Nine entrance petals complete the design. External lighting focused on the uppermost petals heightens the effect of a delicate and yet massive free-floating structure. The nine pools of water are surrounded by walkways, balustrades, stairs and bridges.

The shape of the nine arches is formed by a number of planes, and conical and cylindrical surfaces. The intersections create contours that enhance the arches.

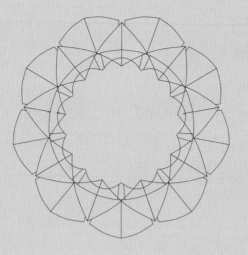

Top View of Entrance and Outer Petals

In conventional structures, dimensions and levels define the elements. In this instance the shape, size, thickness and other details were indicated in the drawings by levels, radii and equations. To achieve parameters that could be understood by site foremen and joiners, a system of coordinates was devised along x, y and z-axes for every 40-degree segment. These coordinates were simplified by working out coordinate levels and distances by which fitters and joiners could arrive at the surface and boundaries. Eighteen reference stations were set outside the building for setting out the arches, entrance, and outer and inner petals. The temple is a marvel of inspiration, engineering ingenuity and exceptional workmanship.

Geometry

The geometry is so complex that it took the design team nearly three years to complete the drawings. The spheres, cylinders, toroids and cones had to be translated into equations, which were then used as a basis for structural analysis and engineering drawings.

The shell surfaces on both sides of the ridge of the entrance and outer petals are formed out of spheres of different radii, with their centres located at varying points within the structure. Each shell has a maximum width of 14 metres and is uniformly thick at 200 millimetres.

The entrance petal is 18.2 metres wide at entrance level and rises 7.8 metres above the podium level. The outer petals are 15.4 metres wide and rise up to 22.5 metres above the podium, and each of the inner petals has a corrugation comprised of a cusp and a valley – that is, an edge and a re-entrance; they rise to an elevation of 34.3 metres above the inner podium at the lowest level.

The shape of the nine arches is formed by a number of planes, conical and cylindrical surfaces. The intersections provide contours that enhance the arches. These nine arches carry the entire load of the superstructure.

For the interior dome, three ribs spring from the crown of each arch. The central rib rises radially towards the central hub and the other two base ribs move away and intersect with other base ribs from adjacent arches, thus creating an intricate pattern.

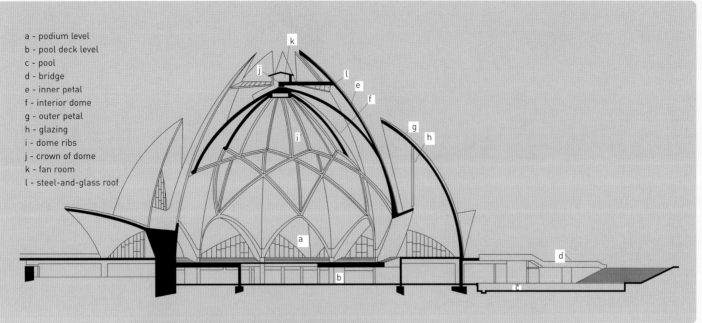

a - podium level
b - pool deck level
c - pool
d - bridge
e - inner petal
f - interior dome
g - outer petal
h - glazing
i - dome ribs
j - crown of dome
k - fan room
l - steel-and-glass roof

Station Points for Setting Out of Arches, Entrance, Outer and Inner Petals

The stations showed here relate to the cusp, re-entrance and edge lines for the entrance, and outer and inner petals. Accurately made curved templates of required radii were then used to develop surfaces between boundaries.

The inner petals hold the interior of the dome in a canopy of crisscrossing ribs and shells of complex design. From the inside, each layer of ribs and petals disappears as it converges towards the top. The radial petals emanating from the inner petals converge at the central hub.

Fariborz Sahba

As head of design teams for different architectural firms in Iran, Fariborz Sahba was involved in the design of a wide range of buildings, including Tehran's Centre of Handicraft Production and Arts Workshops and the Iranian Embassy in Beijing, China. In 1975, he was manager of the design team for the construction of the Nagarestan Cultural Centre, the largest cultural centre in Iran. In 1976 he was selected to design the Baha'i House of Worship for the Indian subcontinent in New Delhi. In 1987, the Institution of Structural Engineers in the UK granted a special award to the Baha'i temple, describing it as: 'A building so emulating the beauty of a flower and so striking in its visual impact.' Also in 1987, Sahba designed 18 monumental terraces as the approach to the shrine of the Bab at the Baha'i World Centre, in Haifa, Israel. International awards include: recognition in 1974 by Iran's Ministry of Housing for his design of a low-cost housing system; the First Honour Award 1987 for 'Excellence in Architecture' from the Interfaith Forum on Religion, Art, and Architecture, an affiliate of the American Institute of Architects; the Paul Waterbury Outdoor Lighting Design Award from the Illuminating Engineering Society of North America in June of 1988; and the GlobArt Award 2000 granted by the GlobArt Academy, Vienna, Austria, for the theme 'Overcoming Religious Barriers'.

Notes

1 In the 11th century, the Seljuk Turks merged with Persian and Central Asian cultures and produced a splendid classical civilisation which, architecturally, gave us the conical dome, the four-*iwan* mosque, and introduced the elements that produced Baroque architecture in 16th-century Europe. This was also the time of al-Ghazzali, of Omar Khayyam and the great mystic and poet Jelaleddin Rumi (1207–73).

2 In western Renaissance paintings, the Assyriac symbolism of sprouting lily buds became the white lily, the fleur-de-lys, symbolising purity and fertility, which the archangel Gabriel carries to the Virgin Mary.

3 The 6th-century Chinese Buddhist T'ien-t'ai classified human experience into states, or 'worlds'. This teaching was adopted and elaborated by Nichiren, who stressed the inner, subjective nature of these worlds. All nine worlds are present in any single world.

4 The essence of the Lotus Sutra says: 'As long as space remains, as long as sentient beings remain, until then, may I too remain, and dispel the miseries of the world.'

5 Suggested reading: The Padmakara Translation Group, *The Way of the Boddhisattva: A Translation of the Bodhicharyavatara by Shantideva,* Shambhala Dragon Editions, 1997. The *Bodhicharyavatara* is a 7th-century text intended for the spiritual development of the Mahayana Boddhisattva.

6 www.bahai.org/article-1-3-2-14.html

7 Baha'i Holy Writings. *ᴀᴅ*

The Built and the Natural Environments: Reaching a State of Positive Coexistence

The Islamic world is a rich 'depository of knowledge' for traditional energy-conservation techniques that have evolved through a great lineage of trial and error. **Mohammad al-Asad** and **Majd Musa** of the Center for the Study of the Built Environment (CSBE) in Amman, Jordan, outline how architects are now beginning to harness their inherited expertise with the aid of modern technologies.

We often underestimate the tremendous influence of the introduction of mechanical air-conditioning and heating systems on the evolution of architecture. Such systems have severed the relationship between the building and its natural climatic environment. Accordingly, both designers and clients have become less concerned about how their buildings relate to factors such as the movement of the sun, direction of the wind and changes in outside temperatures. Mechanical systems, which depend on the ready availability of relatively cheap (usually oil-based) energy, allow for full control of climatic conditions within a building and, therefore, a decision as to whether or not to sheath a building with a curtain-wall glass facade, for example, is unfortunately now most often based on factors unconnected with climatic issues.

Obviously, such an approach is neither sustainable nor responsible. The use of mechanical air-conditioning and heating systems further contributes to carbon-dioxide gas emissions in the environment, thus increasing problems relating to pollution and global warming. It is also economically inefficient and wasteful. In the case of a country such as Jordan, for example, oil is one of its largest import items (representing 8.4 per cent of total imports in 1999), a large proportion of which is used for the purposes of heating and air-conditioning. The more we can limit reliance on mechanical systems, the more we can save on our oil-consumption bills and contribute to limiting a major source of environmental pollution. We also need to keep in mind that international oil reserves will not last for ever; it is expected that known oil reserves will be heavily depleted during the present century.

Interestingly enough, the energy efficiency of buildings can be greatly, and easily, increased at little cost, and in a manner that does not negatively affect our lifestyles. Moreover, achieving such efficiency does not necessitate the use of technologically complex, untried and experimental gadgets, but can be realised through incorporating a number of traditional premodern heating and cooling systems that are very much in tune with nature. In premodern times, people had no choice but to live in harmony with nature. Natural forces were too powerful for available technologies to tame or keep at bay. In this context, the traditional architecture of the Islamic world, which extends over a wide geographical area with various climatic conditions, such as the moderate, the hot and humid, the moderate tropical, and the predominant hot-dry climates, has always been able to effectively respond to its natural environment.

The energy efficiency of buildings can be greatly, and easily, increased at little cost, and in a manner that does not negatively affect our lifestyles. Moreover, achieving such efficiency does not necessitate the use of technologically complex, untried and experimental gadgets, but can be realised through incorporating a number of traditional premodern heating and cooling systems that are very much in tune with nature.

Achieving energy-efficient, climatically interactive architecture incorporates a series of tracks. One involves the effective use of landscaping. This includes the use of plants, which may reduce outdoor temperatures by 5°C through the shade they provide and through the transpiration process, in which plants draw enormous amounts of heat from the air.

Hassan Fathy, New Gourna Village, Luxor, Egypt, 1953
Above
The project employs the indigenous building materials and techniques of mud-brick construction to create high thermal-capacity walls and roofs that regulate the temperature inside the structures in the hot-dry climate.

TR Hamzah and Yeang, Menara Mesiniaga Building, Kuala Lumpur, Malaysia, 1992
Opposite
The Menara Mesiniaga Building ingeniously employs advanced building techniques and modern building materials in an environmentally responsive manner. It effectively introduces the concept of the planted courtyard into multistorey buildings.

Today, we in the Islamic world are fortunate in being the beneficiaries of technologies that allow us to effectively heat or air-condition a space of any size. However, we also have at our disposal a depository of knowledge regarding energy conservation, inherited from centuries of trial and error, and of patient evolutionary practices. Our task today is to bring modern technologies and knowledge in tune with such practices to develop solutions that provide us with economical, sustainable buildings that interact and are in harmony with natural climatic conditions. Such solutions can easily bring about savings of between 20 and 80 per cent in the heating and cooling costs of buildings.

The challenge is to create structures that remain warm in the winter and cool in the summer. Keeping a building warm in winter includes bringing in the winter sun, keeping heat in and the cold winds and temperatures out. In the summer, this includes keeping out the summer sun and heat, and bringing in the cool breezes. Of course, not all regions have cold winters and hot summers. For example, tropical locations, such as those of southern Sudan and Malaysia, have more or less the same climate year round, and desert locations, for example those of the coastal areas of the Arabian Peninsula, have pleasant winters yet unbearably hot and humid summers.

In other words, there are no universal solutions for developing climatically sensitive buildings; what is appropriate in one climatic zone may not necessarily be appropriate in another. Even within a given climatic zone, one needs to identify local conditions and microclimates, including the study of prevailing winds and breezes, and various microclimates created as a result of surrounding buildings or topography. Identifying regional and local climatic conditions is always a most suitable point of departure in attempting to create an energy-efficient building.

Achieving energy-efficient, climatically interactive architecture incorporates a series of tracks. One involves the effective use of landscaping. This includes the use of plants, which may reduce outdoor temperatures by 5°C through the shade they provide and through the transpiration process, in which plants draw enormous amounts of heat from the air. Some plants also work well in controlling the elements in both hot and cold seasons. Deciduous trees provide shade that protects the building from the hot summer sun, but allow the sun to reach the building in the winter. A row of evergreen trees serves as an effective windbreak that protects the building from the cold winter winds, and also serves as a filter for air, particularly in regions that experience summer sandstorms. Deciduous vines are also effective as sun-control devices, and have traditionally been used in overhead trellises, and for fencing.

A modern example in which planting has been used effectively is the Menara Mesiniaga Building (completed in 1992) in Kuala Lumpur, designed by TR Hamzah and Yeang, and winner of the Aga Khan Award for Architecture (AKAA). In this high-rise office building, planting has been used in the building's courtyards to create a 'vertical landscape', thus providing shade as well as cool, oxygen-rich air.

Water bodies may also be used to regulate temperatures in hot-dry climates, since hot air loses heat to water through the evaporative cooling process, and thus gains humidity. Water has always been an important feature in the traditional landscapes of Islamic regions, though not abundantly used due to its limited availability. In this context, traditional courtyard houses generally were provided with water fountains, and palaces often included the delicate flow of water through their courtyards. A notable example of the elaborate, climatically responsive use of water in the traditional architecture of the Islamic world is the 14th-century Alhambra Gardens in Granada, Spain.

A second track in achieving energy-efficient, climatically interactive architecture involves the use of appropriate materials for buildings, including their foundations, floors, walls and

roofs. For example, the use of high thermal-capacity materials for walls and roofs provides thermal masses that regulate the temperature within structures located in hot-dry zones. The mud, mud and straw, adobe or stone walls of traditional buildings of Islamic regions have served as thermal masses by limiting the penetration of heat from the sun during the daytime, and returning this heat to the outside during the night.

Traditional building materials have been used in a few contemporary buildings, such as Hassan Fathy's New Gourna Village project (constructed between 1946 and 1953) and the AKAA-winning Halawa House by Abdel Wahed El-Wakil in Agamy (completed in 1975), both of which are in Egypt. Modern building materials also may be used to achieve energy-efficient buildings. In this context, relatively thick concrete walls may also serve as thermal masses. Furthermore, certain modern materials and building practices allow us to create airtight buildings that limit the transfer of heat between inside and outside, achieved through the use of insulation materials such as polystyrene panels and fibreglass wool.

Modern building materials include low-emissive glass, as well as double- and triple-pane windows, all of which work better than high-emissive glass and single-pane windows in terms of controlling the entry of the sun and heat transmission. However, such advanced glazing technologies do not justify the inappropriate use of large glazed curtain-walls, often without adequate sun-break devices, for the facades of buildings in hot climates; for example, many of the high-rises in the Persio-Arabian Gulf region not only allow the sun in, but also contribute to the problem of excessive heat gain in their surroundings through reflecting the sun's rays. Modern glazing technologies work best when incorporated within environmentally sensitive designs. In the high-rise building of the National Commercial Bank of Jeddah in Saudi Arabia, designed by Gordon Bunshaft of Skidmore, Owings & Merrill (SOM) and completed in 1983, glass areas were reduced and located along the shaded walls of the building's courtyards, thus dealing effectively with the city's harsh summers.

The use of steel, aluminium and glass in the Menara Mesiniaga Building is a good example of the use of advanced building techniques and modern building materials in producing environmentally sensitive buildings in the Islamic world. Another successful example is the use of steel supports covered by tents made of Teflon in the AKAA-winning Hajj Terminal at the King Abdulaziz International Airport in Jeddah (1982), designed by Fazlur Khan of SOM, which has resulted in considerable reduction in outdoor temperatures.

One also may consider materials or building components that may be used at a certain time of the

Choosing appropriate building materials for floors also should be considered. For example, the use of stone, marble or terrazzo floors provides cool surfaces that are very appropriate for hot climates. Of course, they can be adapted to cold climates by covering them with carpets. Before the introduction of central heating, families in a city such as Amman, Jordan, which is hot and dry in the summer, but cold and rainy in the winter, would cover floors with carpets in the winter and remove them in the summer.

day (or season), but removed at another. Shutters provide a simple solution, since they can be opened and closed as the need arises to regulate the entry of the sun. Traditionally, *mashrabiyyas* (grilled wooden window screens) have been used to control the entry of the sun, and there are many examples of them around the Islamic world. *Mashrabiyyas* have been used successfully in some modern buildings, for example in Abdulbaqi Ibrahim's Center for Planning and Architectural Studies in Cairo, Egypt (1979) and Jafar Tukan's AKAA-winning SOS Village in Aqaba, Jordan (1991).

Choosing appropriate building materials for floors also should be considered. For example, the use of stone, marble or terrazzo floors provides cool surfaces that are very appropriate for hot climates, and can of course be adapted to cold climates by covering them with carpets. Before the introduction of central heating, families in a city such as Amman, Jordan, which is hot and dry in the summer, but cold and rainy in the winter, would cover floors with carpets in the winter and remove them in the summer. Consequently, not only the thermal properties, but also the visual quality of the interiors changed between seasons.

One also needs to work within existing construction practices to identify the materials and methods of construction predominant in a given area. It is always wise to work within such systems and to improve and develop their efficiency, rather than to attempt to completely replace them. On a related note, solutions need to be economically sustainable; if changes in building materials and techniques are to be made in order to save energy, it should be possible to recover, in a reasonable time span, the extra costs brought about by using those materials and techniques through additional energy savings. For example, in the case of the National Commercial Bank of Jeddah, considerable energy efficiency has been achieved through the use of the common construction arrangement of a steel structure walled with insulated, marble-finished precast concrete panels.

A very important path that needs to be followed for the creation of climatically sensitive buildings is that of building design. This includes issues such as building form, plan layout, orientation, size of windows, and so on. In this context, it is especially important to apply the principles of passive solar design.

> The location and size of windows is extremely important. Some experts go as far as rejecting the placement of windows in any exposure except for the southern, since southern windows easily can be treated to allow in or keep out the sun, as needed. Northern windows receive little or no sun, and therefore work well in the summer, but allow for high levels of heat escape during the winter.

For example, in the northern hemisphere, a building should be provided with a predominant southern exposure, which is accomplished through placing the building along an east–west axis (with a tolerance of no more than 10 degrees off this axis). Southern exposures are the most efficient for capturing the low sun throughout the day during the winter, and blocking the high summer sun during the summer. This may be achieved through planting deciduous trees along the south of the building (as mentioned above), and providing southern windows with overhangs to allow the low winter sun in but keep the high summer sun out. The ubiquitous use of overhangs in traditional buildings in Islamic areas has always provided buildings and urban spaces with shade.

Here, it should be remembered that since warm air moves upwards, high spaces are easier to cool naturally than are spaces with low ceilings. This partly explains the ubiquity of high ceilings (often combined with small openings just below them) in traditional buildings located in hot climates, such as in many regions of the Islamic world, and low ceilings in the traditional architecture of cold climates. A modern example that benefits from this concept is shown in the high ceilings, particularly at the upper floor, of the buildings of DEGW's Arab Petroleum Investments Corporation headquarters in al-Khobar, Saudi Arabia.

The location and size of windows is extremely important. Some experts go as far as rejecting the placement of windows in any exposure except for the southern, since southern windows can easily be treated to allow in or keep out the sun, as needed. Northern windows receive little or no sun, and therefore work well in the summer, but allow for high levels of heat escape during the winter. Eastern windows allow the hot morning summer sun to enter. The worst in terms

Other forms of climatically responsive traditional buildings also exist in some regions of the Islamic world. These include the traditional tower house in Yemen, where the rooms are arranged vertically, reaching a height of seven storeys, and where buildings are grouped and even butted together with their southern facades exposed to the sun. This protects them from winds and the western and eastern sun, and keeps them cool during the hot summers, in contrast to the modern arrangement of dispersed high-rises.

of energy efficiency are western windows, which are exposed to the hot afternoon sun in summer, and also face the cold, western, winter winds. Windows are the areas in the building where most heat transfer occurs; even double-glazed windows allow five times more heat transfer than a typical masonry wall. Generally, it is recommended that the size of southern windows is limited to 7 per cent of the floor area of a space (in some cases this may be increased up to 12 per cent). If it is necessary to place windows facing other directions, for example to provide for ventilation or light, their size should be limited to 4 per cent of the floor area of the space for northern and eastern exposures, and to 2 per cent for western exposures.

It is worth mentioning here that in the traditional architecture of the Islamic world, careful attention is paid to the location and size of windows in order to regulate the circulation of air through buildings and the entry of the sun into them. This is evident in the placement of openings in the walls bordering courtyards, in allowing for cross ventilation and in the use of high-level windows to let the hot air out. Also, *shukhshaikhas* (clerestory windows) were commonly used as wind and breeze regulators, as in many of Cairo's traditional houses.

A rather sophisticated traditional approach to building in the hot climates of the Islamic regions is the use of wind towers, which are found in the Gulf region where they are known as *badgirs*. These are often tall structures that extend above the roofs of buildings; they have openings on one or more sides, depending on the direction(s) of the prevailing winds and breezes. Wind towers catch the wind or breeze and direct it into the interior of the building. Due to the high thermal capacity of their walls, they cool off at night but also remain relatively cool in the daytime. Air cools off when it comes in contact with the walls of these towers and then enters the building. In some cases, particularly in hot-dry regions, air coming through a wind tower into the interior of a building passes over a water surface, or possibly damp pieces of cloth, to further cool off and gain humidity.

Building form and plan layout contribute to the creation of climatically sensitive buildings. The arrangement of building components around courtyards is a common plan layout of traditional buildings in Islamic regions, and the role of courtyards as temperature regulators has been extensively dealt with. Today, examples of climatically sensitive uses of courtyards include the AKAA-winning Saudi Ministry of Foreign Affairs in Riyadh (1984), designed by Henning Larsen; the SOS Village in Aqaba; National Commercial Bank of Jeddah; and the Menara Mesiniaga Building in Kuala Lumpur. Whereas the first

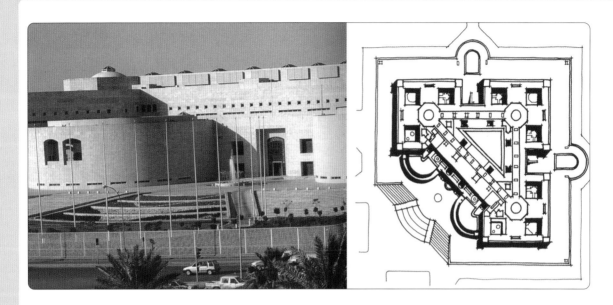

Opposite
The use of wind towers
(*badgirs*) is a traditional,
climatically responsive
approach to building in hot
climates of the Islamic world,
particularly in the Gulf region.
Wind towers catch the wind or
breeze through their openings
above the roof level; air cools
off when coming in contact
with the walls of the towers
and descends to the interiors
of the buildings. The photo
shows wind towers at the
traditional Mojtahedzadeh
House (now used as a school)
in Isfahan, Iran.

**Henning Larsen, Saudi
Ministry of Foreign Affairs,
Riyadh, Saudi Arabia, 1984**
Above
The introverted plan layout of
the building presents a good
example of the climatically
sensitive use of courtyards in
the modern architecture of the
Islamic world.

two buildings adopt the more-or-less conventional courtyard arrangement, the last two effectively reinterpret and reintroduce the concept of courtyard into high-rise buildings.

Other forms of climatically responsive traditional buildings also exist in some regions of the Islamic world. These include the traditional tower house in Yemen, where the rooms are arranged vertically, reaching a height of seven storeys, and where buildings are grouped and even butted together with their southern facades exposed to the sun. This protects them from winds and the western and eastern sun, and keeps them cool during the hot summers, in contrast to the modern arrangement of dispersed high-rises. Of course, in terms of energy efficiency, a multistorey building is better than a single-storey one, since each storey protects the one below it from heat escape in the winter and from heat gain in the summer. However, this statement is not necessarily an endorsement of high-rise buildings, as the higher floors would be susceptible to high-speed cold winds in the winter. Moreover, only the lower floors of a high-rise would benefit from the use of landscaping as an energy-saving tool, unless the landscaping were incorporated into the building, as at Menara Mesiniaga.

Urban fabrics affect the degree to which buildings may achieve energy efficiency. Obviously, the more it is possible to physically connect buildings, the better those buildings are able to function together as one unit in terms of climate control. Under such circumstances, each building would provide the adjacent building with additional protection from the elements. For example, the compact urban form of old Islamic cities in hot-dry regions, such as Cairo, Damascus and Jerusalem, where often there are no setbacks from one plot to the other, and no exposed facades except for those facing adjacent streets, is a good example of buildings functioning together as elements of climate control. On a related note, the narrow streets often found in such traditional cities also provide sensitive climatic solutions since they limit the penetration of the hot summer sun into the space of the street, and allow the street to remain in shade during much of the day. However, urban arrangements in modern cities in the Islamic world, with their dispersed buildings (often glazed high-rises) and wide streets, are climatically inappropriate.

On a related note, the narrow streets often found in such traditional cities also provide sensitive climatic solutions since they limit the penetration of the hot summer sun into the space of the street, and allow the street to remain in shade during much of the day. However, urban arrangements in modern cities in the Islamic world, with their dispersed buildings (often glazed high-rises) and wide streets, are climatically inappropriate.

One effective approach to environmental control involves considering changes in the utilisation of spaces to respond to daily and seasonal microclimates. This arrangement is common in Islamic regions. In traditional houses in Old Tunisia, as well as in other historic Islamic cities such as Damascus, people use the roofs at night in the hot summers, and the lower storeys of their two-storey houses during the day, when the high thermal mass of the walls provides protection from the hot sun.

Another route towards achieving energy-efficient, climatically interactive architecture is the use of buffer zones. Various building spaces may be used as buffers for other spaces in the building. For example, a space to be used primarily during the night might be used to block the sun from a space primarily intended for use during the day. Covered porches are excellent examples of such buffer spaces, as is the use of arcades around the courtyards in traditional Islamic architecture. And there are modern examples of this utilisation of buffer zones, such as in the placement of the services, including toilets, staircases and elevators, at the eastern side of the Menara Mesiniaga Building, and in the use of a double-skin roof for the buildings of the al-Khobar headquarters of the Arab Petroleum Investments Corporation.

One effective approach to environmental control involves considering changes in the utilisation of spaces to respond to daily and seasonal microclimates. This arrangement is common in Islamic regions. In traditional houses in Old Tunisia, as well as in other historic Islamic cities such as Damascus, people use the roofs at night in the hot summers, and the lower storeys of their two-storey houses during the day, when the high thermal mass of the walls provides protection from the hot sun.

Finally, sources of renewable energy also need to be considered. Here, solar energy immediately comes to mind. As is common in Jordan, solar energy can be used to heat water for washing or bathing, and in some cases it can also be used to heat interior spaces. Of course, solar energy may also be used to create electricity through photovoltaic cells. The AKAA-winning Barefoot College (1988 and ongoing) in Tilonia, Rajasthan, India, by Barefoot Architects, is completely dependent on photovoltaic solar panels to generate the energy required for night lighting and for water pumping.

The cost of installing photovoltaic solar systems has been, until recently, prohibitively expensive, but this cost is now coming down, and such systems are becoming increasingly competitive with other means of generating electricity. In some areas, authorities require electricity companies to allow for the linking of the electricity grid to buildings powered by photovoltaic solar systems, and thus electricity may be exported from the building to the grid during off-peak hours, and from the grid to the building during peak hours. The advantages of photovoltaic systems, once their prices become fully competitive, are tremendous. They are pollution free and, further, they provide a decentralised means of generating energy for individual buildings, and give inhabitants more control over access to energy sources.

Although we have not yet fully succeeded in producing architecture that is completely independent of fossil fuels, there are promising examples in the contemporary architecture of the Islamic world that demonstrate the possibility of creating buildings that effectively

incorporate various principles of energy efficiency. But unfortunately, such practices are not widespread. Architects and engineers in Islamic regions need to undertake further research and experiments regarding the creation of energy-efficient buildings. And the general public, who represent the clients and users of the buildings, need to be educated on the significance of energy-efficient building.

In addition, governmental institutions involved in the construction industry must be encouraged to rethink existing building codes and regulations in a way that would enhance energy-efficient building. It is worth mentioning here that a number of governments have begun to address the issue of energy efficiency in buildings, but in a rather generalised manner. For example, in Dubai the use of glass for the facades of buildings has recently been controlled by building regulations stating that specific percentages of glass area to facade area should not be exceeded. The regulations also require the use of double- or triple-glazing in some cases. However, such an initiative is only a step along the long road to energy-efficient building.

In Jordan, at the Center for the Study of the Built Environment (CSBE) we have begun a process aimed at further exploring the creation of energy-efficient buildings that are in tune with their natural surroundings. The process has been initiated by a public competition for the creation of a low-income, water- and energy-conserving housing unit in the city of Aqaba, Jordan's only port city. The competition was organised in cooperation with the Aqaba Special Economic Zone Authority (ASEZA) and the Water Efficiency and Public Information for Action programme (WEPIA), which is being carried out in association with the Jordanian Ministry of Water and Irrigation, and funded by the United States Agency for International Development (USAID). The Aga Khan Award for Architecture has also provided additional support.

It is hoped that the competition will provide a catalyst for instigating a more ambitious programme for the development of energy-efficient buildings in Jordan. It aims at developing guidelines that would be placed on the CSBE website (www.csbe.org) and therefore made easily accessible to designers, contractors, students, property owners and the general public. Further goals are to implement such guidelines through the construction of energy-efficient buildings, ranging from small houses to apartment buildings to schools, in association with partners who may include public-sector organisations, nongovernmental organisations and individuals. The project provides a natural and integral extension of the CSBE's pre-existing projects on water-conserving landscapes and grey-water reuse. ⌀

Although we have not yet fully succeeded in producing architecture that is completely independent of fossil fuels, there are promising examples in the contemporary architecture of the Islamic world that demonstrate the possibility of creating buildings that effectively incorporate various principles of energy efficiency. But unfortunately, such practices are not widespread.

Opposite
The climatically sensitive, multistorey approach to building is traditionally known in the Islamic world. In the traditional tower houses of the old city of Sana'a, Yemen, the rooms are arranged vertically and the houses reach a height of up to seven storeys. The tower houses are grouped or even butted together with their southern facades exposed to the sun. Thus they are protected from winds and the western and eastern sun, and remain cool during the hot summers.

The Architecture of
Mimar Sinan

The distinguished Turkish architect **Turgut Cansever** remembers the work of Mimar Sinan, the celebrated 16th-century Ottoman architect who sought the Divine in Reason and Beauty, and whose work unified both in its aesthetic and functionalism.

Each work of art comes into being as the unity of a message; thus, through the ages, in their quest to attain this wholeness, Islamic works of art have followed Islam's fundamental precept: convey the message, then cease; that is, do not carry on, do not insist. With their scrupulous timidness, with their quiet restraint, Islamic works have been designed to glorify their message. In the architecture of Mimar Sinan, the 16th-century master architect of the Ottomans, this quest achieves some of its finest flowering. This short essay is an attempt to understand the rationale that underpinned his preferences.

Born in 1489, Sinan was conscripted into the sultan's service in 1512, having become acquainted with Islam's mystical tradition, Sufism, during his education. As a member of the Ottoman infantry, a janissary, he became a military engineer and gained the opportunity to design and build ingenious structures such as bridges, and ships for the army on its way to conquest. It was during his service that he developed his deep knowledge of Abbasid, Fatimid, Mamluk, Persian and Seljuk architectural heritages.

'I saw the monuments – the great ancient remains; from every ruin I learned, from every building I absorbed something.' So says Sinan in his autobiography, *Tezkiret-ul Bunyan*, dictated to his friend, the poet Mustafa Sai Çelebi. Sinan died in 1588 at the age of 99 after completing numerous architectural works – some sources mention 477 – most exhibiting rich improvisations of his preferences.

Here, in a brief overview, we will try to understand his approach, at the same time seeking to deepen our understanding of Sinan the man, and so shed light on – indeed, even question – the artistic works of our own era.

The Tradition Behind Sinan's Design Concept
Sinan was deeply influenced by the variety of architectural interpretations he observed in different parts of the Islamic world, and by their underlying unifying, fundamental Islamic stylistic features, and especially by the Seljuk and early Ottoman architectural achievements. These works of architecture, which stand independently in space, their parts functioning as independent elements within infinite space, together constituted a great collectivity of tectonics creating an

When we look at the 16th-century Ottoman world, we see that Islamic mysticism – Sufism – defined and governed all decisions so that they were made in accordance with accepted spiritual values and preferences. In this context, Ottoman architecture, as sacred art, became another mode of declaring the Islamic concept of *tawhid* – unity of God, unity of existence. It is the manifestation of total surrender to God's will; an order where everything is in its rightful place; acceptance that everything on earth, every spot and every moment is a manifestation of sacred existence.

ornamental unity. Here, ornamental unity does not imply ornamentation as a decorative addition to the surface; rather it describes a design method that incorporates repetitive elements, resulting in an ornamental whole.

His was a unique approach, finding its sources first in the nomadic cultures which tried to record their observations of their ever-changing environment, eyes constantly moving, questioning the individual's place in the world, and then in Islam, declaring the sublimity of the individual. In Sinan's architecture, we find their reflections realised as a continuous attempt to resolve the controversial elements of existence – juxtaposing the sublime and the modest, the plain and the ornamental, the grand and the small-scale, the complex with the simple – sequences of architectural forms as pillars, domes, arches which set in train an effect of motion through their harmoniously changing dimensions.

The observer is prompted to ask: What governed Sinan's decisions regarding the arrangement of such a varied spectrum of similar but, at the same time, strikingly different architectural structural elements, which he chose to organise into such intricate yet deftly conceived work.

When we look at the 16th-century Ottoman world, we see that Islamic mysticism – Sufism – defined and governed all decisions so that they were made

Mihrimah Sultan Mosque, Istanbul, 1542

Opposite
Between the madrasah and the mosque there is a thicker minaret, an axis around which an ingenious solution was developed for creating an expression of motion, as if the mosque is turning towards the valley on the right.

Mihrimah Sultan Mosque,
Istanbul, 1542
Above
Above the very dark shadows of
the wide entrance eaves, the
building loses its relationship with
its foundations, in a seeming
advance towards the sea.

and submission to the divine will. Each stage was thoroughly learned so that its precepts could be applied in everyday life and reflected in the works of the artist. Only after each stage had been successfully mastered was it possible to pass to the next. Sinan's experience of this strict religious discipline is naturally mirrored in all of his works.

Those behaviours, feelings and expressions as defined by Sufism were the spiritual states, *ahwal*, that guided and dominated Sinan's approach; feelings such as modesty, respect, simplicity, a social conscience, an eye to the future, the attempt at monumentality on a human scale; joyous colours, brightness and tranquillity of movement are all evident. Using materials and technologies naturally, according to their potential, without concealing them, was a tradition closely followed by Sinan. Wood and stone, metal and tile were used together, reconciling the natural and the man-made, emphasising their coexistence in a respectful manner. Nothing jarred, nothing was exaggerated; every part played its appropriate role, excluding all fethishising tendencies. *Tawhid* (unity of existence) established unconditional submission to God's will, while setting the foundations for a feeling of security, and was reflected as polychromy, brightness, clarity and tranquillity of movement; harmonising with attitudes of sublimity, respect, simplicity, responsibility. All these facets coalesced, contributing to the achievement of monumentality on a human scale, a harmonious realisation of the sublime unity.

The Prophet's command, 'Look at everything. Look at the sun and the stars in the sky. Look at the stone on the ground', was a dictum followed by Sinan that enabled him to improvise brave designs through his evaluation of the unique, historic, local conditions, limitations and potential of each site. He conceived three alternative planimetric architectural schemes, in each case executed after he had worked from a different perspective.

Below we will examine four of his numerous achievements: Mihrimah, Shehzade, Süleymaniye and Selimiye, and in so doing attempt to gain an insight into his thinking.

Mihrimah Mosque, Istanbul, 1542

Sinan's Mihrimah Sultan Mosque was an attempt to develop a dynamic unity in an asymmetrical landscape. Here, the site posed a challenge. The mihrab wall skirting the steep slope terminates the interior space. The thick, powerful entrance facade wall, its huge sustaining arch carrying the central dome, is pierced with windows. The transition space in front of the mosque has been eliminated, merging interior with

in accordance with accepted spiritual values and preferences. In this context, Ottoman architecture, as sacred art, became another mode of declaring the Islamic concept of *tawhid* – unity of God, unity of existence. It is the manifestation of total surrender to God's will; an order where everything is in its rightful place; acceptance that everything on earth, every spot and every moment is a manifestation of sacred existence. Consequently, we can say that Sinan's works should also be numbered among the corpus of sacred art – art that embraces the Islamic spiritual states – which led him to choose from among the rich and complex diversity of formal expressions to develop a unity as a reflection of *tawhid*.

The mystical education Sinan underwent was oriented to develop the individual's attitudes and behaviours along a progression of different stages, among them the acquistion of piety – that is, being close to reality; the teaching of sincerity (the knowledge to eliminate error);

exterior. The static immovable central dome is positioned on the axis of three semidomes. Similar in plan to the mosques at Bursa Yesil and Yildirim, here the two lateral semidomes transform the square plan into a rectangle, parallel to the mihrab wall. Because of the asymmetrical organisation of three semidomes and an imposing wall on the fourth side, the main dome is no longer at the centre of the cubic volume of the exterior unity. Consequently, one gets the feeling that the entire space is advancing towards the Bosporus, away from the slope.

Approaching the mosque from the coast, the eye is caught by a thicker minaret on the northeast side that reinforces this sensation of movement towards the madrasah, while the upper structure seems to float above the wide eaves that cast their deep shadow below, the structure an immaterial being seemingly suspended from the sky, not touching its base.

Shehzade Mosque, Istanbul, 1543

After the death of Süleyman's beloved son, Sinan worked on the Shehzade Mosque. It is the first of his famous trio, Shehzade and

Shehzade Mosque, Istanbul, 1543
Right
The ornamental carvings, the repetitive floral friezes seen at Shehzade, aimed to create a heaven in memory of Sultan Süleyman's son, Mehmet.

Below
Shehzade Mehmet's tomb. The use of coloured stones further accentuated this attempt to create a heaven on earth; all the elements declare man's mission to beautify the world for which he is responsible.

Süleymaniye in Istanbul, and Selimiye in Edirne.

The highest point of the historic peninsula within the city walls, situated between the Fatih and Beyazid mosques, the site was selected so that the mosque casts its silhouette right in the centre of the axis between the Golden Horn and the Sea of Marmara.

If one considers the plans and concepts governing the design of space in earlier Ottoman mosques – Yildirim and the Old Mosques in Bursa; Uc Serefeli and Beyazid mosques in Edirne; and Fatih, Beyazid and Sultan Selim mosques in Istanbul – Sinan's Shehzade Mosque provides a new solution; a natural outcome of an understanding of the site with its very central position. The ensemble of a main dome, four semidomes, eight smaller semidomes and small corner domes creates a noble quality. Here, the mosque's relation to its foundations is disguised by an eave set over the main entrance and a series of shaded porches with elegant arcades.

Shehzade Mehmet's tomb is within the complex; adorned with red stones, the tomb ornaments the garden surrounding the mosque, so that it becomes Shehzade's heaven.

Like Sinan's other works, Süleymaniye is an open-ended, ornamental unity of architectural tectonics; the interior becomes a continuation of the infinite space. Thus the structure, with its arches, pillars, domes, minarets and balconies, becomes a unity of a transcendental system. The harmonious coexistence of autonomous elements and solutions lies at the very heart of Sinan's projects.

Süleymaniye Mosque, Istanbul, 1557
Süleymaniye Mosque followed Shehzade. Construction began in 1550 and reached completion in 1557. It was built at the west end of the Old Palace, on the highest edge of the steep slope, parallel to the Golden Horn. The addition of Süleymaniye's silhouette beside those of the Hagia Sophia, Beyazid, Shehzade and Fatih mosques was a stroke of genius – a monumental contribution. Following the Islamic tenet that man can reach perfection only when he has attained complete knowledge, the mosque is encircled by madrasahs (schools) for religious sciences and mathematics.

In the upper structure are two semidomes; one above the entrance, the other above the mihrab; then two huge lateral arches carrying the central dome. The whole composition is radically different in the sense that, with its lateral leaping arches, Süleymaniye stretches from west to east in the direction of the holy kiblah (Mecca), parallel to the Golden Horn. Four minarets are placed around the latecomers' courtyard; the two on the main entrance wall of the mosque, with three balconies, are higher than the other two, with their two balconies. The design, a deliberate attempt to accentuate the lateral movement, parallel to the Golden Horn, is in studied contrast to Hagia Sophia's static, heavy, robust architectural expression.

On either side, below the leaping arches, the walls are again pierced by windows and the building is enlarged as it descends towards ground level; a reinterpretation of the pillared mosques of earlier periods, where space is elongated parallel to kiblah. With the addition of repetitive windows at eye level, the effect of lateral expansion is emphasised once more. The Muslim at prayer, turning to right and left, is conscious of a sense of ever-extending, infinite space.

Like Sinan's other works, Süleymaniye is an open-ended, ornamental unity of architectural tectonics; the interior becomes a continuation of the infinite space. Thus the structure, with its arches, pillars, domes, minarets and balconies, becomes a unity of a transcendental system. The harmonious coexistence of autonomous elements and solutions lies at the very heart of Sinan's projects.

Selimiye Mosque, Edirne, 1575

Selimiye Mosque, which Sinan called his masterpiece, was built for Sultan Selim, another of the sons of Süleyman, between 1569 and 1575. Like a precious cut gemstone, it is situated on a rocky formation at the highest point of Edirne, almost at the midpoint of an infinite, huge Thracian plain stretching away to the Balkans. Its four minarets are positioned around a large central dome, which can be seen from all parts of the city – a glorious monument.

The windowed wall enclosing the courtyard at Süleymaniye conceals the mosque's relationship with the ground; at Selimiye, above the level of the women's balconies, the structure has been transformed into a system of domes, arches and other buttressing elements so that it seems detached from its foundations. Similar to Mihrimah, both mosques appear to

float in the air, but the methods used to achieve this end differ markedly.

At Selimiye, such a treatment of the upper structure diminishes the effect of the height of the cubic base. The supporting structural elements have vertical, curved, inclined forms according to their functions. A pervasive dignity is expressed through the dynamic unity of these forms; thus we find ornamentalism, the collective unity of all.

Eight pillars carry an octagonal drum, which in turn carries the central, gigantic dome. However, it is interesting to note that four of the octagon's pillars – two at the entrance and two in front of the mihrab niche – are almost buried. The remaining four descend freely to the floor on either side, once again creating a rectangular plan parallel to kiblah, and accentuating the effect of lateral expansion at eye level.

The mosque incorporates a unity of structural elements at five levels: the central dome; its octagonal drum, with semidomes on four sides; the mihrab semidome and the square plan; the rectangular plan at the level of the women's balconies and imperial pew; and, finally, the rectangular plan of the ground floor parallel to kiblah. Forty windows pierce the octagonal drum of the dome, transforming it into a totally independent yet all-embracing entity. The dome seems to hang as if suspended from above.

In addition to the eight pillars carrying the dome, eight arches buttress the octagon; the outward thrust of the corner semidomes is controlled by the four minarets at the corners. Consequently, we are again confronted by an outwardly extending solution, the height of architectural sophistication; here the exterior is the reflection of the interior, the interior the reflection of the exterior.

Walls, or the cut stones constituting walls, can be perceived by the naked eye. All of the architectural elements exist with their boundaries, each cut stone carefully placed to accentuate the reality of the wall as a plane. Arches and domes clearly reflect their structural purposes without reverting into a show of power and grandiosity. Together they constitute the collectivity of ornamental elements in infinite space. Such a unity is one completely at odds with the organic concept of unity of the Renaissance and Baroque. Forty windows on the octagonal drum; *muqarnas* as transitional elements to the dome's circular base; arches with coloured stones; the changing dimensions of architectural elements, such as the strikingly narrow stairways leading to the women's balconies – together they constitute the ornament elements, each with its individual existence within the totality, yet another reflection of Islam's conception of attaining sublimity through individuality.

As God's caliph in the world, the Muslim knows his responsibilities and has the right to develop his consciousness of existence freely. Here, architecture becomes a means to develop such an impartial entity, which itself is a particular realisation of the architect's own intuition.

Sinan's Genius

Each of Sinan's works contains different layers of meaning that can be perceived selectively, whether by the trained eye or the untutored mind.

Awe, devotion, patience and contemplation are other aspects of what governs architectural preferences in Islam. Purity and clarity of form, and a confident, conscious and responsible approach to architecture, enable the realisation of a sublime work.

In such a context, where both architect and future users are Muslim, the architect does not strive to orient, dominate or impress the pious. The building is never an element of ostentation.

Grandiosity, arrogance, an exaggerated sense of compassion, humility and perfection are foreign to this atmosphere.

As God's caliph in the world, the Muslim knows his responsibilities and has the right to develop his consciousness of existence freely. Here, architecture becomes a means to develop such an impartial entity, which itself is a particular realisation of the architect's own intuition.

Thus, Sinan's architecture is indeed a projection of Islamic cosmology. It is a means to beautify the world, a reflection of Islamic belief and consciousness, Islamic *ahwal*. His architecture is humble and natural, neither dramatic nor insistent; it seeks to beautify and ornament. Explicit, lucid, real, in continuous motion yet tranquil; here nothing is disguised.

Today, living in chaotic times, surrounded with all the chaos of architectural experimentation that seems to be lost and without any fundamental roots, we believe it is our duty to ask: 'What is the role of mankind in the world?'

'Man's mission is to beautify the world' – so spoke the Prophet Mohammed. Love for beauty has been the governing wisdom of every stage of Sinan's designs.

Intention is the beginning of all. ⌂

Biography

Mimar Sinan was born a Christian, in Agirnas, in the centre of Anatolia, in 1489, and lived to the age of 99. As he grew up, he learned from his father how to work with stone and timber, and went on to become a stonemason. In the summer of 1512, when he was 23, he joined the Ottoman infantry as a janissary, converted to Islam, and studied mathematics and carpentry at Enderun, an elite school for the chosen few. He served as a military engineer in four of Sultan Süleyman's campaigns, during which time he worked on projects that included converting churches into mosques, the construction of a bridge across the Danube, and shipbuilding. He built his first mosque whilst general of the janissary engineers at Aleppo.

Sultan Süleyman appointed Sinan as chief of the imperial architects in 1538, after which, with Haseki Hurrem Camii, he built Istanbul's first *kulliye* (complex of buildings adjacent to a mosque), for Süleyman's wife, Roxelana. According to some sources, this was followed by nearly 500 further structures.

In all, before his death in 1588, Sinan served four sultans: Selim the Grim, Süleyman the Magnificent, Selim II, and Murad III.

The Use of Geometry in Islamic Lands

'Architecture only truly qualifies as "Islamic" if it displays significant ornamentation.'
Dr Keith Critchlow, the professor emeritus of the Visual Islamic and Traditional Arts department of the Prince of Wales Institute of Architecture, who runs his own architectural practice on authentic design principles, explains the significance of geometry in inherited Islamic scholarship, and how it might be applied today.

The first principle in approaching Islamic architecture and its decoration is to remove ourselves from our habitual views about decoration, and even to a degree remove ourselves from our habitual definitions of architecture, at least for a sufficient time to allow different criteria and intentions to be considered.[1]

The word 'architecture' is laden with preconceptions and associations, whoever defines it. Clearly, however, there is a significant difference between a finely built mosque or madrasah and the typical humble, yet completely functional and adequate, Islamic village dwelling. The difference is not so much 'in the eyes of God' as in the eyes of people, particularly the wish of Muslim communities to express in their public buildings their gratitude to their Creator.

So, to arrive at a more accurate definition of Islamic architecture, we first need to look deeply into the meaning of Islam itself, so as not to miss the most vital point of definition. To be too summary would be a serious error, but there is always a profound simplicity to the Revelation of Islam that affects every corner of Islamic life. This is the doctrine of unity: 'Say God is One.' Secondly, one must take into account the injunction upon believers to pray five times a day – at least. This means that whatever space a Muslim has to live in, it needs to accommodate oriented space in which to pray. This is a primary requirement for any Islamic building. At another level, Islam means living 'the will of God' – the holy Koran spelling out what this entails morally.

In this brief article we would like to uncover other dimensions to Islamic understanding (which SH Nasr

The word 'architecture' is laden with preconceptions and associations, whoever defines it. Clearly, however, there is a significant difference between a finely built mosque or madrasah and the typical humble, yet completely functional and adequate, Islamic village dwelling. The difference is not so much 'in the eyes of God' as in the eyes of people, particularly the wish of Muslim communities to express in their public buildings their gratitude to their Creator.

has called 'sacred science'): an objective view of the 'created order' that embraces a theocentric perspective, that is, a Creation with a Creator.[2]

This brings us to the inheritance of Islamic scholarship and the sources of the scientific studies that were available to Islam from earlier civilisations. The fact that the greatest 'teacher of teachers', Ibn 'Arabi, was called Ibn Flatun (son of Plato), was an important philosophical reference to the Hellenic sacred sciences inherited by those who wrote about 'why the ancients allotted the solid figures to the elements'[3] – clearly indicating the study of Plato's *Timaeus*. The Brethren of Purity, an anonymous group of 15th-century Islamic scholars, assembled a remarkable and encyclopaedic volume of work based on Pythagoric/Platonic influences.

For the Muslim, to be in harmony (at one) with the Creation means being able and educated to know what are the fundamental patterns that make the Creation a cosmos rather than an accident. Thus, Ibn 'Arabi taught that without pattern there can be no meaning. Or, put another way, 'meaning' arises within us only when we can recognise the pattern. Not a word of this article would be understood if you – the reader – were unable to recognise the patterns the letters make for each word – if you will forgive the obvious. This universe is a shared pattern.

Thus cosmos is pattern and, thereby, is wholeness; and, as Socrates says in the *Republic,* to Glaucon and the others gathered –

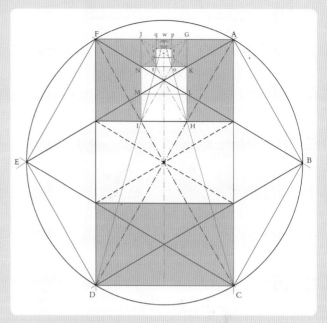

to learn arithmetic and geometry is the surest way to rekindle the 'eye of wisdom ... an eye worth 10,000 of your fleshly eyes'. Thus, through the influence of Plato, the power and reverence for geometry, as significant pattern, was deeply embedded into the minds of Muslims and, therefore, their educational curriculum. Outwardly, the observation of the 'points of light' in the night sky was the other 'science' so assiduously studied – particularly as it was the main source of security of navigation for the caravans of the desert who travelled by night. The whole of the modern world inherited the science of astronomy due to the great practitioners of Islam and their transmission of the knowledge of the

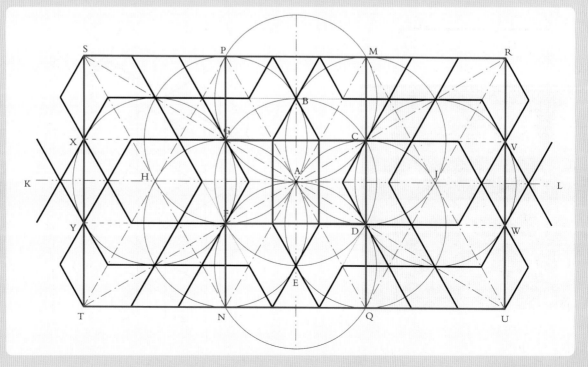

Above
Hexagon within circle with Radius = 1: a root 3 rectangle naturally divides into three of itself proportionally. This is unique amongst all rectangles.The root 3 (√3) rectangle is a natural product of the hexagon, which is the most natural division of a circle. If the edge of the hexagon is 1, then the rectangle through is √3 in breadth.

Right
Red = the √3:1 proportional rectangles, which are three in one: the black lines show both the construction (circles) and the lines of the finish's *zellij* (geometrical mosaic tilework) pattern.

The Holy Prophet (Peace be upon Him) discouraged representational art by saying to the artists: 'Yes, you can paint or make images of living creatures – if you can make them breathe.' This directed Muslim artists to look to the inner objective, 'formative' forces that lay behind, within or under the surface of the living world; and so the patterns of geometry and the serpentine forms sometimes called *islimi*, sometimes called arabesque, sometimes called biomorphic, and sometimes vinomorphic, were adopted, forming an objective supranatural language of art forms.

ancients. This is clearly evidenced by the names of Arabic origin we have for so many of the stars and constellations.

So Islam inherited the four essential art/sciences of Pythagoreanism, and welded its own unity of knowledge in a form that SH Nasr has called Abrahamic Pythagoreanism. The four art/sciences were: arithmetic as pure number; geometry as number in space;[4] music as number in time; and, finally, astronomy (or cosmology) as number in space and time. These were the objective languages that were universally available and, for the Muslim, represented 'patterns of the Divine Mind' as expressed in the Creation.

The Holy Prophet (Peace be upon Him) discouraged representational art by saying to the artists: 'Yes, you can paint or make images of living creatures – if you can make them breathe.' This directed Muslim artists to look to the inner objective, 'formative' forces that lay behind, within or under the surface of the living world; and so the patterns of geometry and the serpentine forms sometimes called *islimi*, sometimes called arabesque, sometimes called biomorphic, and sometimes vinomorphic,[5] were adopted, forming an objective supranatural language of art forms. Thus characteristic sinuous Islamic art forms are not derived from imitating nature, but rather by 'seeing within' nature, using the eye of wisdom.

When we look at Islamic patterning, it is wisest to seek the quest for cosmic order that lies within it.[6] This we will give a few examples of. No science, ancient or modern, sacred or secular has attempted to explain cosmology without arithmetic or geometry. Even the six 'days' of Creation – with their hexagonal implications – are held equally sacred by Judaism, Christianity and Islam.

Islamic artists saw the way of achieving four levels of meaning in one artistic effort: first, the significant common language of geometry; secondly, the integral patterns of the heavenly rhythms of the cosmos (the 12 houses of the zodiac – the number symbolism of all the planetary rhythms); thirdly, the achievement of the delight in the harmony of symmetry together with decorative coloured effects to lift the spirits;[7] and fourthly, the achievement of patterns of cosmic meaning that integrated different symmetries. This was done in such a sophisticated manner that it has taken until modern times for 'Western' physicists to recognise that fivefold symmetry can cover

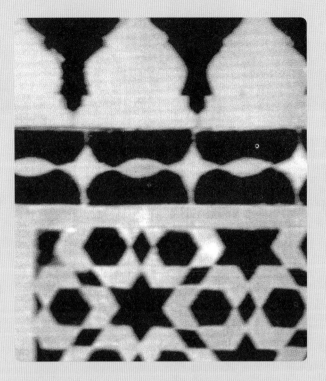

a two-dimensional surface without leaving any 'odd' spaces; even Kepler only arrived at the most simple pentagonal dual tiling, whereas the Muslim genius uncovered the principles of the so-called 'Penrose rhombs' centuries ago, creating extraordinarily beautiful and sophisticated masterworks.

Thus Islamic architecture fulfils its spiritual role by exhibiting beautiful patterns integrated into the forms of unity so essential to all Muslims – specifically the form of the dome. It further elaborates upon these with 'cosmos-reflecting' patterns of orders within orders. It fulfils the objective scientific role of displaying the objective ground of beauty, and fulfils the social role of cohering a theocentric society by reminding it to recall its final destiny and pray regularly. This is achieved by seeing the patterns that 'decorate' the elevations of so many beautiful Islamic buildings as following the shapes of the prayer mat – thereby reminding the faithful to pray and recall their relationship with God (zikhr).

The achievements of Islamic architecture at the level of 'environmental wisdom' have been well covered by such as Hassan Fathy, yet never lose sight of the ultimate purpose and destiny. Industrialisation and its inevitable 'love child', computerisation, have both had the disastrous effect of putting forward 'worldly' arguments and definitions of 'economy' that are materialistically based, thereby divorcing the builder of the body from the builder of the 'soul', and thus leaving communities in the conceptual quagmire of 'comfort zones' of trivial television and complete forgetfulness of the grandeur of a civilisation, let alone a purpose to life. However, there is still a choice, despite the materialist onslaught within the traditional world of Islam.

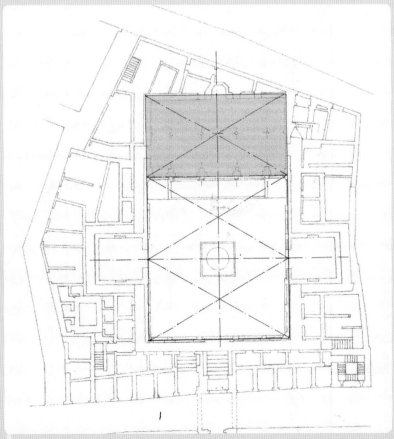

Below
The concept and fact of 'mean orbit' refers to the adjustment of the distance travelled by each planet from the elliptical to the circular, which reflects the 'perfect' archetype. Note there is no change in the distance.

Understanding will always be the key to peaceful coexistence; the recognition that all of us have a common fate, and that each of us is interdependent. Thus, to reiterate the importance and significance of Islamic pattern we need to have a broad, as well as a deep, view of the totality of the situation. Indeed, architecture only truly qualifies as Islamic if it displays 'significant' ornamentation.

When it comes to ornamentation in Islamic architecture, what is the basis upon which choice or judgement can be made? And how many contemporary architectural practices understand and use ornamentation authentically?[8]

Each of the Abrahamic traditions has an 'inner', as well as an 'outer', aspect of meaning. We are all only too well aware of the use and misuse of 'claimed' outer aspects of the different faiths, but the only essential and lasting value lies within the harmony of the inner teachings of all three faiths – and these require diligent seeking.

There is little likelihood that anyone can truly say that they understand the value and meaning of Islamic art unless they have a knowledge of the inner wisdom of the practitioners. These are invariably found to be in the Sufi orders of each region or school.[9] The Islamic craft guilds were, and are, understood as 'participation in the will and law of God', thereby tracing a path to

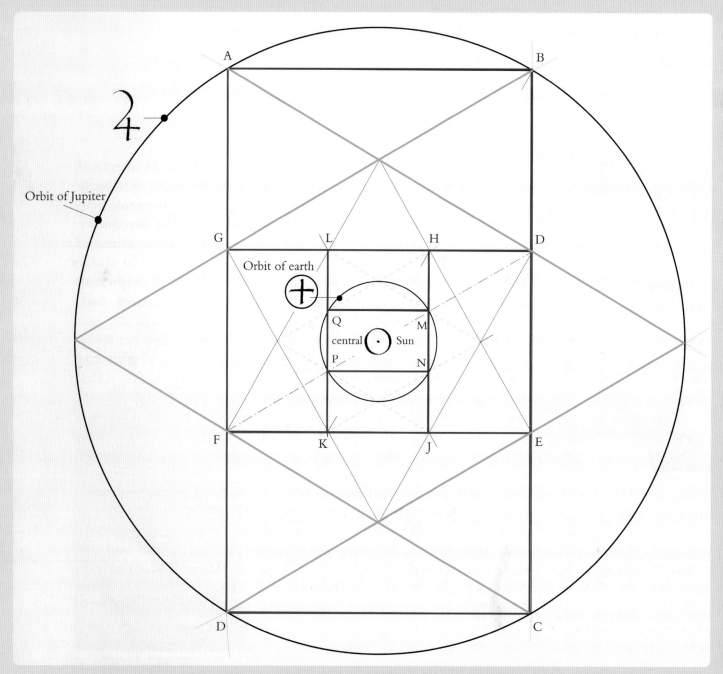

Orbit of Jupiter

Orbit of earth

central · Sun

Above
Shapes A, B, C, D, E, F are
those that can fit together to
make a fivefold continuous
grid on a two-dimensional
surface. The pentagon, or
regular fivefold shape, will not
on its own close-fit to make a
two-dimensional surface. This
was the discovery of the
Muslim geniuses and the basis
of their many wondrous
fivefold patterns.

'truth' through the cathartic and purifying act of following a craft discipline. Industrialisation and computerisation have not only become the biggest threat to the 'art' that is ultimately the 'ascent' of the soul, but have also enticed the 'sharper' members of so many Islamic communities to finance seeking alone – faster, with less effort, and inevitably exploiting others. This is precisely the contrary purpose of a sacred science and a sacred tradition. Thankfully there are a few centres, albeit more hidden than openly seen, that are keeping the flame alive and producing art and crafts of great beauty.

To reinforce the depth of the inner teachings of Islamic Sufism we will cite the prayer blessing of 'Abd al-Aziz al-Mahdari, who was one of the teachers of Ibn 'Arabi. This prayer blessing has 24 aspects.

Each of the 24 blessings is direct, simple, unambiguous and obviously devout in intent. However, if we wish to penetrate a little deeper into how essentially innocent and powerful in their simplicity such prayers are – and how they affect those who use them – we can find the commentary by Pablo Beneito and Stephen Hirtenstein,[10] the translators of these prayer blessings, most helpful; their theme is 'depth within depth' and 'pattern of meaning within pattern of meaning'.

Number 10 in the set of 24 blessings is arranged around a single root letter as a principle of unity. They unfold into three deeply significant aspects of the Creator: divine generosity (jud), being (w'jud) and existence (m-w-jud). Thus each profound aspect is to be found

one within the others. This expresses not only three ontological degrees, but equally three aspects of the 'Muhammadan Reality', these being: innermost meaning (sivv), revelation (mazhav) and concealment (khizana).

So not only is there pattern within pattern, but deeper meaning within deeper meaning! This is, however, a subject of participatory study, not mere theoretical fascination. The principle involved is a doorway into an appreciation of ornamentation in Islamic architecture. A traditional saying recorded of the Prophet (Peace be upon Him) is translated as: 'God is Beautiful and loves Beauty.'

In summary:

• The first principle of all three Semetic Abrahamic faiths or revelations is that we all live in the same cosmos. This cosmos means an objective order – moral, harmonic, mathematical and human. This common cosmos is a 'creation' achieved in six 'days' for all three faiths.

• At the root of the creation is 'pattern', for without pattern there is no perception or intelligibility. The word 'pattern' originates from the same Latin root as 'Father' (pater); again, a common appellation for the Creator.

• From the traditional perspective, human birth entails forgetting. This is a common doctrine inasmuch as prayer is remembrance, or zikhr, or, for Plato, anamnesis. Thus pattern in Islamic art and architecture holds at least a threefold value, reminding us of theological, anthropological and cosmological meaning. Geometry integrates all three without interfering with their hierarchy.

• Islamic wisdom (tawhid) is 'pattern within pattern'. We have presented here a series of examples in the language of geometry and geometric pattern, as utilised by the Islamic architectural tradition. We trust that the evidence is self-demonstrating, objective and hopefully food for consideration. ∆

Notes
1 Interestingly, the equivalent to our word 'architect' in Islam is mohandis, which means geometer, thereby making both structure and ornamentation integral.
2 As opposed to the currently fashionable 'Big Bang' theory and its accumulation of what are purported to be a series of chance accidents (which conveniently avoids addressing the issue of causation).
3 Al-Kindi, who was considered at the time of the Italian Renaissance to be one of the world's 10 greatest minds.
4 This is the subject of the author's book Order in Space, Thames & Hudson (London), 1969).
5 The very fact that there are so many different English words used demonstrates the difficulty of the English language in expressing metaphysical realities. For the Muslim craftsmen we spoke to, islimi was perfectly adequate.
6 See, for example, the author's Islamic Patterns (Thames & Hudson, 1976).
7 Colour was not primarily seen as an aesthetic (hedonistic) experience, but rather like the music of the spheres in sound, each colour holding a planetary meaning. (See N Ardalan and L Bakhtiar, The Sense of Unity: The Sufi Tradition in Persian Architecture, University of Chicago Press, 1974; John Gage, Colour and Culture: Practice and Meaning from Antiquity to Abstraction, Thames and Hudson (London), 1995).
8 The architectural practice the author runs is one of the few that uses authentic design principles.
9 We are grateful to Dr Hajami of Fez for many of the insights indicated.
10 See the Journal of the Ibn 'Arabi Society, Vol. XXXIV, 2003.

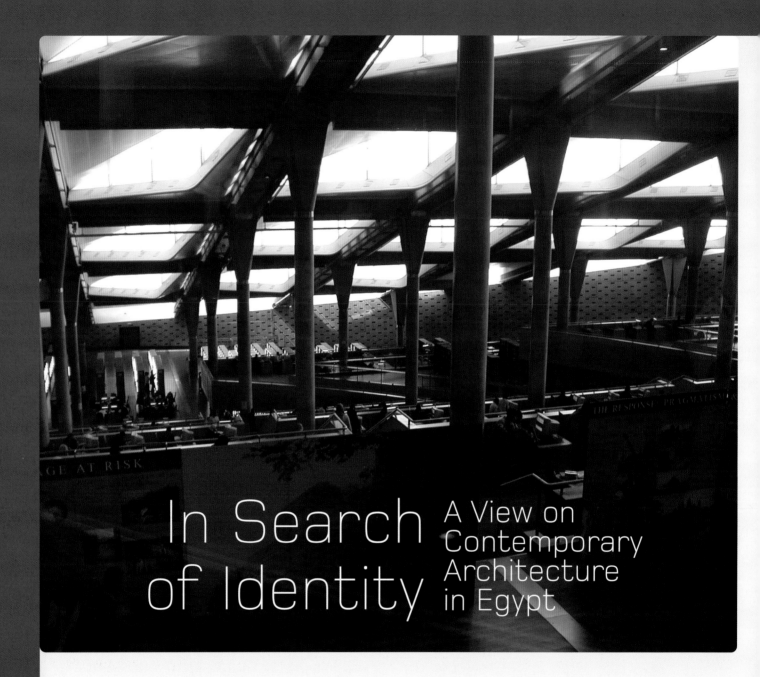

In Search of Identity

A View on Contemporary Architecture in Egypt

Some 15 years on since the death of Hassan Fathy, contemporary Egyptian architecture is 'struggling' to find a consistent approach. **Mohamed El-Husseiny** describes four projects, including his own Oteiba House, that may point a way forward.

From the colossal Pharaonic monuments of ancient Egypt, to the elegant Arab/Islamic buildings of the Middle Ages and Renaissance, and from chic, ornate French and Italian turn-of-the-century buildings to modern-style office buildings and five-star hotels, Egypt has it all. One would think that contemporary architects in a country with such a rich and inspiring architectural heritage would have little difficulty in producing excellent architecture. And yet architecture in Egypt is struggling.

As we enter the 21st century, architecture in Egypt still seems to be fluctuating undecidedly between the adoption of Western models, as a vehicle conveying notions of modernity, affluence and efficiency, and a return to traditional historical and vernacular models as a statement of national pride, confirming and conserving the country's heritage.

Throughout most of the 20th century, Egyptian mainstream architects, as well as the general public seemed, to a large extent, to disengage themselves from the architectural models of their local heritage, which they considered outdated, inferior and no longer able to cope with modern requirements, and instead gravitated strongly towards Western concepts of progress and efficiency. But by the mid-20th century, this notion began to be challenged. The increased awareness of the possible role of traditional/ historic architectural elements and concepts in contemporary designs was mainly pioneered and championed by the late Hassan Fathy.

From the 1940s, through his now famous New Gourna project,[1] Fathy demonstrated that traditional building forms, spatial configurations and construction methods can, in certain cases, provide an economical, practical, aesthetically pleasing and culturally compatible alternative to imported Western models. At the time, Fathy gained the respect and admiration of only a few dedicated believers, and it was not until his work was recognised internationally, and he had received a number of prestigious international awards – including the Aga Khan Award for Architecture in 1980 – that his work began to be recognised locally. Subsequently, this and various other regional vernacular and neo-historic styles were revived and, fuelled by a wish to confirm an independent identity, gained increasing momentum within the Egyptian architectural community.

With a number of notable exceptions, both schools of thought have been marred by superficial and commercialised imitations of their most popular and defining forms and elements. In all too many cases, these elements have been used only as icons representing certain perceived values or connotations, without true consideration for their compatibility, effectiveness or sustainability. Fortunately, as we mature culturally and learn more from past experiences, an increasing number of architects (and clients) are coming to appreciate that this practice is no longer acceptable. Many are finally reaching the inevitable conclusion that serious research, analysis, evaluation and objective implementation of compatible and sustainable design elements, from both local and imported models, are necessary to synthesise a new, complex-free, modern Egyptian architecture of which we can all be proud. However critical one may be of the current state of affairs, there is, undeniably, a multitude of positive examples giving good reason for optimism and shining a light at the end of the tunnel. Below are a selection of projects that represent the major directions and methodologies used in this quest in search of identity.

Snøhetta, Bibliotheca Alexandrina, Alexandria, 2002

The commission for this building was awarded to the Norwegian architects Snøhetta, on the strength of their prize-winning entry for the 1989 international competition for the design of the new Library of Alexandria. Snøhetta worked in collaboration with the Egyptian engineering firm Hamza Associates on the construction of the building, which began on site in 1995.

Built very close to the original site where the historic Library of Alexandria once stood, the new Bibliotheca Alexandrina is a landmark building. Destined to carry the burden of reviving the spirit of a grand historic monument in a modern context, it is an appropriate representation of the challenges now facing Egyptian contemporary architecture.

The building's main feature is the slanted disc-shaped roof, emerging from the ground. The high-tech roof is divided into cells, intelligently designed in the abstracted shape of human eyes and eyelids to allow the natural light to filter into the grand reading hall below. The reading hall, divided into seven terraced levels following the inclination of the roof above, enjoys excellent light quality, which is comfortable and pleasing.

Although the size of the building is grandiose at 160 metres in diameter, and 11 storeys high, it is by no means overwhelming. With four storeys below ground substantially reducing its perceived height, a gently inclined slanted roof, deceivingly simple facades and a wide piazza, the building appears light, uncomplicated and inviting.

The shiny slanted disc symbolising the rising sun, the tall elegant internal columns flared at the top in an abstract interpretation of the famous lotus columns,

Snøhetta, Bibliotheca Alexandrina, Alexandria, 2002

Opposite
The main building, in the form of a slanted disc symbolising the rising sun, is a modern interpretation of a classic icon. It is a truly modern building that within its structure has successfully blended the essence of its heritage.

Below
Lotus columns support the slanted roof with intelligently designed 'eyes' filtering natural light into the grand reading hall below. The quality of light inside the reading hall strikes just the right balance between a soft, relaxing atmosphere and sufficient lighting for reading.

Rami El Dahhan and Soheir Farid, Kafr El-Gouna, Red Sea coast, 1992–98

Above
A delightful introduction to Egypt. The reception building of the Sultan Bey Hotel at Kafr El-Gouna embodies layers of development and refinement in a traditional vernacular architectural model and proves that it is still compatible with modern requirements.

Right
Recreating the traditional souk or khan. The shopping arcade at Kafr El-Gouna – a curving pedestrian spine – offers a cool, shaded reprise from the heat and glare outside and adds a sense of romance, anticipation and discovery.

and the inscribed granite external cladding, are unmistakable references to ancient heritage and pedigree. But there is no doubt that this is a modern building exuding excellence in design and construction. Except for inadequate visitors' parking, it seems to function very well, both as a practical building and a cultural landmark. But the most important achievement of this design is, as described by the director of the Bibliotheca Alexandrina, Dr Ismail Serageldin, to have 'successfully avoided the twin dangers of ossified copying of the past, and cultural inappropriateness'.[2] It is an example of a truly modern building that within its structure has successfully blended the essence of its heritage.

Rami El Dahhan and Soheir Farid, Kafr El-Gouna, Red Sea coast, 1992–8
Faithful to Hassan Fathy's style (itself a development and refinement of the original Nubian architecture), the architects of these hotels, residential apartments and

commercial spaces, which form part of the
El-Gouna holiday village, have successfully
propagated the natural warmth, intimacy,
spontaneity and human scale of the vernacular.
Skilfully adapted to the tourist-resort model, this
is, for foreigners, a delightful introduction to
Egypt. For Egyptians, it is an inspiring model for
many villages, small towns and local communities
across the country. Through serious study of
their buildings' type morphology and the
environment in which they were to be built, the
architects have crafted beautiful traditional
architectural forms (domes, vaults, arches and
timber latticework) embedded in a harmonious
dialogue of interesting spaces, and pleasing
vistas in a sound and sustainable urban entity.

In addition to substantial economies in
construction cost, the use of local materials and
traditional building techniques added familiarity to the
buildings. The value of this familiarity is that local users
and visitors can easily appreciate the possibility of
replicating this model, in whole or in part, in their own
local communities. The project is a tribute to how well
an undiluted traditional system can continue to serve
the needs and requirements of a modern community.

Dr Abdul-Halim Ibrahim, Palace of Arts, Cairo, 1998
In the heart of Cairo, amidst preciously scarce gardens
and greens, the new art gallery for the Ministry of
Culture is located within the complex of the old Cairo
Exhibition Grounds in Guezira. Designed and built in
the 1940s, and with many subsequent additions, the
complex – no longer used for exhibitions, and now
a centre for the arts – includes a variety of
architectural styles, but is mainly dominated by the
neo-Islamic style of the original 1940s exhibition

A series of steel trusses carries a translucent Plexiglas roof over the entire hall, conveying a sense of openness and filling the space with a soft natural light that is as pleasing and inviting as the cool courtyard of a mosque on a warm summer's day.

Dr Abdul-Halim Ibrahim, Palace of Arts, Cairo, 1998

Above
Functional and entirely modern: under a clear Plexiglas and steel truss roof, air-conditioning ducts, lighting and audio-visual equipment float, freely exposed, above the main gallery, making a clear statement.

buildings and the new Cairo Opera House situated almost directly opposite.

Respecting the prevailing theme, yet refusing to be restricted by its constraints, the Palace of Arts seems eager to grasp this unique opportunity and enters directly into an interesting, almost controversial, dialogue with time, culture and the surroundings. Using traditional design and construction elements of Islamic architecture, it connects strongly with the neighbouring buildings. But this is certainly not a 'cut-and-paste' exercise. Arches, *mashrabiyya* (intricate timber screens applied externally to windows) style cantilevered windows, domes, crenellations and screens, and even a minaret, have all been abstracted, modified and reused in a new context evolving beyond the cliché to reflect a notion of progressiveness deeply rooted in tradition.

The double-height lobby, capped by a transparent multifaceted glass dome, is reminiscent of a Mameluk mausoleum, but takes on a new function as a well-lit and welcoming entrance to the building. As one would expect in a prestigious mosque, the small entrance leads into a grandiose space. The unexpected change of scale never fails to grasp the attention and admiration of the visitor, who instead of delving into the grand *sahn* (courtyard) of a mosque, now enters the main exhibition hall of the art gallery.

A series of steel trusses carries a translucent Plexiglas roof over the entire hall, conveying a sense of openness and filling the space with a soft natural light that is as pleasing and inviting as the cool courtyard of a mosque on a warm summer's day. And yet, the architect does not shy away from modern reality, has no false notions of conserving a tradition by freezing it in time and not allowing it to develop and progress, and does not hesitate to use the technology of the day to serve and enhance his building. Air-conditioning ducts, along with the latest lighting and audio-visual equipment float, freely exposed, above the hall, making a clear statement of almost industrial functional Modernism, extremely well suited to the purpose for which the building was commissioned.

A fusion of two seemingly contradictory directions, the building is a bold attempt to achieve a successful symbiotic relationship between old and new, East and West. If not for anything else, then for this alone it deserves to be applauded.

Notes
1 See Hassan Fathy, *Architecture for the Poor: Experiment in Rural Egypt*, University of Chicago Press (Chicago), 1973, previously published under the title *Gourna: A Tale of Two Villages*.
2 Dr Ismail Serageldin, *The Rebirth of the Library of Alexandria*, Bibliotheca Alexandrina (Alexandria), 2002.

Oteiba House, Hurgada

Mohamed El-Husseiny, Oteiba House, Hurgada, 2003
Having been given a considerable amount of freedom in the design stage, the Oteiba House in Hurgada was an opportunity for me to implement many design principles based on the reintroduction and development of elements of traditional and vernacular design in a modern context.

In the hot, dry climate of the Red Sea coast, the traditional entrance courtyard remains one of the most important elements of the house. In contrast to the heat and glare of a harsh, and often uncontrollable, exterior, the protected courtyard, with its (eventual) canopy of natural trees, palms and plants, creates a cool and welcoming transition into the dwelling. The four small fountains penetrating the entrance

floor humidify and add a relaxing sound of water. Rooms and balconies open freely on to this microcosm without sacrificing privacy, and enjoy the pleasing view and microclimate. With small sheltered openings on the harsh south facade, the house now opens to the desirable breeze and panoramic view to the northwest.

Direct descendants of the traditional *mashrabiyya*, simplified timber latticework screens fulfil the same functions at a fraction of the cost and blend with the modern lines of the building

Basic geometric forms and light-reflecting sand-coloured stucco facades convey a sense of environmental consciousness and modern simplicity. Simple square openings substitute for traditional crenellations, while traditional pointed arches anchor the building in its heritage. Δ

Out of Context:

Development and Design in Lebanon

In the wake of the 15-year civil war in Lebanon, reconstruction programmes have favoured rebuilding the physical infrastructure rather than addressing the inequality of development. Hashim Sarkis explains the importance of addressing the inequality between Beirut and rural Lebanon in light of its recent history. He also demonstrates, through his own projects in undeveloped contexts, how it is possible, through partnerships with NGOs and private developers, to encourage programmatic and formal innovation in a way that is potentially transformative.

Housing for the Fishermen of Tyre, Abbassiyah, Tyre, South Lebanon, 2005

Above
Sequence of views showing the road into the project and the public courtyard.

On War and Development

The late historian Albert Hourani has argued that developmental inequality between the city and the country was one of the main reasons behind Lebanon's civil war, which lasted from 1975 to 1990.[1] His diagnosis stands out against the prevalent interpretation of the war as a mainly religious and ethnic conflict. It remains evident today in the deteriorating economic conditions of the region.

Since the end of the Second World War, the physical environment of the Third World has been radically transformed by the drive towards development. An ambition that ran across continents and became the signpost of progress and emancipation, development has reshaped the economic and political, as well as the physical, environments of the Third World in general, and the Muslim world, whether in countries guided by the development strategies of the Bretton Woods Institutions, like those of North Africa, the Middle East and Southeast Asia, or those that were influenced by the planning models of the Soviet bloc, like the Turkic eastern European states.

Development helped introduce electricity, telephone and roads across the territories of nation-states. It also helped modernise, sometimes Westernise, yet often destroy local industrial and agricultural production. Land tenure and population distribution have also been deeply affected. Given the lack of resources in these countries, development policies were hardly ever fully implemented, but their impact on regional territories and their landscapes has been immense.

For the most part, development meant urban development at the expense of the countryside and the environment. After 50 years of accumulated failures, debts, and social and environmental ills, it is easy to criticise this drive. Back then, however, development made sense. It provided collective identity and aspiration to the newly created citizenships. As much as we would like to think of modernisation as the driving impulse behind much of the architectural production of the post-Second World War period, we ought to link this impulse to a much more conscious pursuit of economic progress and social emancipation – to development. This pursuit justifiably persists today, even if the policies and mechanisms of implementation have changed, and even if we continue to uncover inherent contradictions in the very definition of development.[2]

In a small, mercantile country like Lebanon, the state rarely ever extended its role beyond arbitrating between the different sectarian groups. Most development, social and educational programmes were left in the hands of the private sector. Only during a short period in the late 1950s and early 1960s did a 'welfare state' government take on the role of a master planner, and guide many social projects towards half execution. Successive pre-1975 governments favoured a laissez-faire attitude, leaving it to civil society and private institutions to ameliorate living conditions. However, private development shifted the balance overwhelmingly towards Beirut and exaggerated the country/city inequalities that subsequently fuelled, if not triggered, a 15-year war.

The civil war almost annihilated the state and the public's expectations in the few social programmes it sponsored. In the absence of the state, national and international NGOs took over emergency relief, food and medicine distribution. In some cases, these organisations also helped reorganise the institutions of civil society. When the war stopped, the NGOs continued to operate, but they shifted their focus from relief to development projects, particularly in rural areas where state initiative on the development front remains ostensibly absent.

Postwar reconstruction programmes in Lebanon have favoured rebuilding the physical infrastructure over addressing this inequality in development. Redressing socioeconomic inequalities and environmental problems was not a priority of national policy even before the civil war. Despite a political rhetoric that insisted otherwise, the postwar reconstruction and development programmes have also concentrated on Beirut, and have prioritised the reconstruction of the physical infrastructure of the country.

Twelve years after the end of the war, *Wallpaper** magazine may make downtown Beirut look cosmopolitan, but it would have a hard time with a town like Damour, 20 minutes away. Even Beirut's limelight has faded over the past few years. The national debt has risen because of the high cost of physical reconstruction, and an economic recession has paralysed the country since 1996 and led to several waves of emigration. When interrogated, successive governments have argued that this approach to reconstruction is difficult, but necessary to accelerate the pace of development, and that the social benefits and individual liberties that have been sacrificed in the process will be regained once the economy turns around.

As characterised by Amartya Sen, this approach needs to be confronted with another, based on the idea

Agricultural fields

New roads and parcelling

Project

Future development

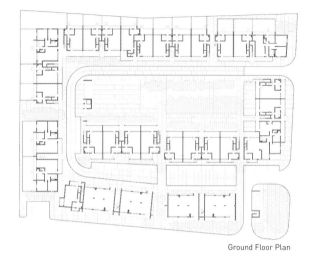

Ground Floor Plan

Second Floor Plan

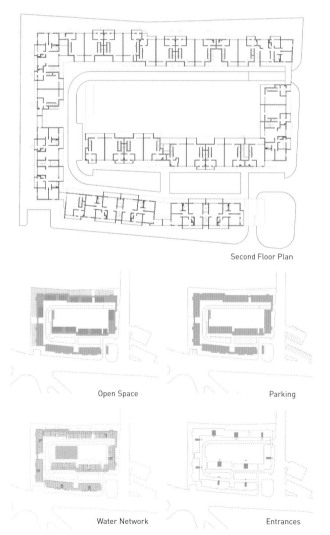

Open Space

Parking

Water Network

Entrances

that development is the means to an end – that of 'expanding the real freedoms that people enjoy'.

In the meantime, the conditions of several disenfranchised groups have been worsening, and those who have not been able to emigrate have started raising their voices. Several NGOs have taken up their causes and have expanded their programmes to involve the communities in determining their needs and helping improve their living conditions. Even private citizens are coming up with innovative projects and unusual collaborations to address local needs.

The three projects that follow have been initiated in these underdeveloped contexts by local NGOs and private developers, sometimes working directly with disenfranchised groups. They represent a range of environmental, rural, urban and architectural issues that extend beyond the usual problems of design and, as such, encourage programmatic and formal innovation. They also represent opportunities for transforming the contexts in which they are located.

The unusual programmes resulting from the exigencies of the different sponsors encourage unusual design responses. Limited resources may limit the design options, but they also lead to a certain level of innovation. Even if an assigned programme is well defined, the design of the building must provide a flexible framework that can anticipate future changes, and future additions funded by future grants.

Teaching at Harvard and working from Cambridge on projects in Lebanon may not seem like an easy arrangement at first, but I have benefited from this physical and intellectual distance, in being able to work on these projects at a production pace that allows for constant modifications and long periods of waiting, while being able to assimilate their design potential as agents of change. These projects, and the desires of their clients and audiences to effect change, encourage less conformist design responses that express the desire to transgress context and to project better futures.

Housing for the Fishermen of Tyre, Abbassiyah, Tyre, South Lebanon, 2005

The fishermen's community of Tyre, a city of 25,000 residents on the southern coast of Lebanon, has been suffering from a housing shortage and overcrowding. Strict preservation laws in this World Heritage city, and a weakened economy, have further limited housing options. Additionally, the sea has not been kind to the fishermen, and the Tyre region has greatly suffered from the successive wars between 1975 and 1990.

In order to reverse their dire conditions and to provide their marrying children with housing, the fishermen formed a housing cooperative and convinced the archdiocese of the city to donate a 6,500-square-metre piece of land in Abbassiyah, on the agricultural fringe of Tyre. They also raised funds from several local and international agencies to build a housing project. In this process, they were assisted by the Association for Rural Development, an NGO whose aims are to 'develop human and natural resources in the rural areas of Lebanon', and help 'social actors to acquire the knowledge and capabilities necessary to the enhancement of their living conditions'.

The new site is an agricultural field surrounded by citrus orchards, a hospital and chaotic, speculative development that mushroomed illegally during the war. Subject to the implementation of a new master plan for the area, the site will abut a new road that will replace the existing agricultural road to link the city with its hinterland. Most of the surrounding agricultural property is already being subdivided for speculative construction, and the site will therefore be one of the few large-scale parcels in the area.

Given the chaotic and unpredictable conditions of the new context, and its isolation from the residential quarters of Tyre, the design defines a strong edge to the outside along the site perimeter. However, it introduces an organisational frame for the surrounding streets and new parcels. This edge is made of an extenuated building (7 metres thick) that wraps in on itself, creating an internal road and an open space. The internal road continues the side street, provides access to the units and connects the two main access points. The open space provides a common public garden and a playground. In order to avoid a closed, urban-block effect, the linear mass is broken down into a series of buildings separated by gaps used for public circulation, providing variety within the building volume. The corners are treated differently in response to varying external conditions.

One of the main concerns of the fishermen was to maintain equality among the units, particularly in terms of access to private outdoor space and access to the views. Thus the units had to be different, depending on their location in plan. The project consists of 80 two-bedroom units, each with about 86 square metres of interior space, and about half the area is private outdoor open space.

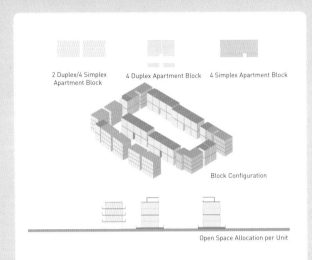

2 Duplex/4 Simplex Apartment Block   4 Duplex Apartment Block   4 Simplex Apartment Block

Block Configuration

Open Space Allocation per Unit

The units are arranged in three types of blocks or groupings. The first consists of simple single-storey flats (simplexes) arranged around a common scissor stair. The second consists of four duplexes, each consisting of an open floor plan for living spaces and a second floor for bedrooms. This type is located around the main open space. All living floors have cross views and cross ventilation, and are extended to the outside by private outdoor spaces (gardens and porches for the lower units, and balconies and roof decks for the upper units). The third type is a combination of duplexes and simplexes, and is located at the corners of the main open space.

One of the main features of this project is the large open space. The space of the building mass in relation to the open space allows for an increasing enclosure and then release. The open space is made of two parts: a paved area with a collective water tank underneath, and a planted area. Rather than framing the parts, trees are used to mark entrances to paths between buildings. The landscape spills through these gaps between the buildings to the exterior, emphasising the connection between the interior open space and the street.

Balloon Landing Park, Beirut, 2005

With the deteriorating economic and political situation in the Middle East, and 10 years after the reconstruction process was initiated, much of the new land cleared for development in downtown Beirut remains empty. This has led the property holding company developing the downtown to rent out some parcels for temporary use, for example as basketball courts and nurseries, as well as this project for a tethered helium balloon that rises as high as 300 metres to allow a formidable view of downtown Beirut.

Housing for the Fishermen of Tyre, Abbassiyah, Tyre, South Lebanon, 2005

Opposite
Plans: the wrapping form of the housing creates a hierarchical continuity among the open spaces. Private open spaces surround the court, and parking, building entrances and water distribution follow the hierarchy set by the wrapping form. The open space is half planted/half paved, in order to create a temperature differential to generate air circulation. This is further enhanced by the thinness and openness of the living spaces.

Above
Model.

Above right
Block configuration: the blocks surrounding the inner court consist of four duplexes: two with gardens and two with roof decks. Each unit has an outdoor area equal to half its size.

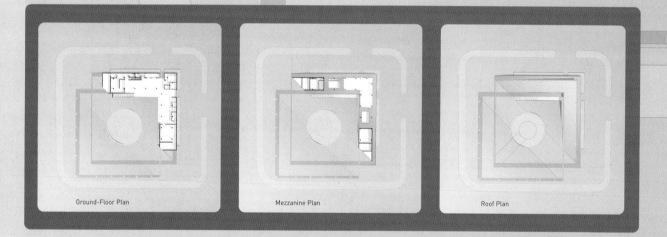

Balloon Landing Park, Beirut, 2005

Below
Plans sequence: the sectional intersection of the different levels, and the multiplicity of ground planes in the project, is registered in the reverberating squares of the top view plan. On the ground(s), the edges of the squares demarcate the circulation zones and weave the different levels.

Ground-Floor Plan

Mezzanine Plan

Roof Plan

Rather than flattening the diagonally skewed ground and encumbering it with kiosks, taking away the power of the emptiness and the potential of using the area surrounding the balloon, the design lifts the ground and places the waiting areas, restaurants and entertainment underneath, while the ground is cleared as park. The different planes of the project interpenetrate both sectionally and planimetrically. As seen from the ground, and from the sky, the reverberations of the square figure intensify the void.

With respect to the question of development, the above projects share a common formal strategy: the way that they extend from their internal order to the outside world, projecting how an internal visual and formal order could spill out to inform the world outside.

In this way, we move from a negative definition of development to one that maintains the idea of potential, nonclosure, participation, experimentation, and of imagining alternatives: not one developing world forced to follow predetermined models and frameworks, but many worlds contributing to what Amartya Sen has described as an expanded definition of development. In this case, development is expanded to include the built environment that could play a bigger role in imagining better futures without imposing them. These better futures could be defined as a form of context transgression, an underlying common ambition among NGOs and the regions in which they operate.

Context transgression deserves a closer examination because it questions one of the main assumptions about architecture in the developing world – its link to regionalism. Regionalism, as a conscious undertaking, started in Europe with the Romantic impulse to reject the rationalist universalism of the Enlightenment in

favour of more emotional, regional and, later on, nationalistic views of the individual. A parallel Darwinian meaning was attached to this idea when Patrick Geddes brought it into urbanism and proposed, in his famous valley section, that human settlements and land-use patterns should be designed to fit the characteristics of the ecological regions in which they occur.[3] In the US, Lewis Mumford and Clarence Stein sought refuge in the naturalness of the region, as a harmonious and spiritual finality, away from the artificiality and politics of the city. With the emergence of nation-states, particularly after the Second World War, every other nation sought to identify its vernacular building style as a source of Modern architecture, at once legitimising its adoption of modernity and its own existence as a geopolitical region.

In a more recent revival, regionalism has been given a critical posture against globalisation, by Tzonis, Lefaivre and Frampton, who argue that critical architecture at the edges of the Western world resists globalising tendencies by juxtaposing within the same structure regional architectural qualities (indigenous materials and landscape) against universalist Modernist features.[4]

Critical regionalism has been one of the most influential means by which the recent production of architecture in the developing world, especially in the Middle East, has been explained. While it takes on the difficult task of reconciling Modernity with tradition, this kind of regionalism misses out on the fact that its critical endeavour still takes place within the larger socioeconomic framework of

development. It also misses out on the possibility that the reverse posture – context transgression – could itself be an important local aspiration or expression of tradition. Traditions, as Hobsbawm reminds us, are constantly being created and transformed.[5]

For all of the above, we have to move from region as a naturalised entity to one where the region is the provisional but more adequate scope of understanding and charting the dynamic networks of development. We have to move from a view of developing countries as static regions, physically and temporally external to the Western world, and see them as distinct but evolving settings for societies that are pursuing development with different means. It is the misunderstanding of other societies as fixed and inherently different that has helped misinterpret today's unfortunate events as a clash of civilisations.

Alternative environments could emerge and alternative models of freedom, tolerance and democracy could propel them. Between the universalist tendency to encapsulate everything under one large collective human drive, and the regionalist tendency to fragment the world into particular and self-fulfilling mini-worlds, there is a broad spectrum of possibilities waiting to be explored. △

Above left
View of the platform looking northwest towards the hotel district and the sea.

Above right
View of the balloon from the entrance. On the inside, the yellow balloon is visually clipped by a sectional compression in order to enhance the ascension.

Notes
1 Albert Hourani, 'Ideologies of the mountain and the city', in Roger Owen (ed), *Essays on the Crisis in Lebanon*, Ithaca (London), 1976.
2 Amartya Sen, *Development as Freedom*, Anchor Books (New York), 1999.
3 Alan Colquhoun, 'The concept of regionalism', in GB Nalbantoglu and CT Wong (eds), *Postcolonial Space(s)*, Princeton Architectural Press (New York), 1997, pp 13–23.
4 See, for example, Kenneth Frampton, 'Towards a critical regionalism: six points for an architecture of resistance', in Hal Foster (ed), *Anti-Aesthetic. Essays on Postmodern Culture*, Bay Press (Seattle), 1983, pp 16–30.
5 Eric Hobsbawm and Terence Ranger, *The Invention of Tradition*, Cambridge University Press (Cambridge), 1983.

Contemporary Architecture In Turkey: An Evaluation

Turkey has carved out its own position in the architectural world. While engaged and competing with the West, it has also sought out its own identity and never lost sight of its architectural values. Doğan Tekeli outlines the main strands and leading figures in Turkish architecture, highlighting how its contemporary culture is indebted to a process of modernisation that took place very much on Turkey's own terms.

For many years, Turkish architecture has not been considered worthy of extensive evaluation, viewed as it was within the generalised context of pluralistic Islamic architecture. At the beginning of the 20th century, Turkish art historian Celal Esat Arseven and architect Kemalettin rewrote the history of Turkish architecture, maintaining that it was a distinct genre in its own right. Although contemporary Turkish architecture has largely broken with its past, it continues to be evaluated within the realm of Islamic architecture. Yet among today's non-Western architectural traditions, it deserves particular attention because, with the possible exception of Russian architecture, it was the earliest that aspired to be Modern.[1]

Modern architecture was established in the first half of the 20th century with the claim of universality and creativity as its success criteria. The claim of universality dissolves the importance of time and place. On the basis of this assumption, an architecture regarded as 'non-Western' can be evaluated according to the criteria of abstract universality and originality, and yet the diversity within the Modernist genre is denied. This denial demeans the claim of universality in time and place, and the search for abstract originality becomes impossible.

The exclusion of local distinctions from the claims to universality of Modernist architecture is striking. Studies evaluating the architectural performances of peripheral countries ignore the contextual conditions of architectural practice. This results in a search for marginal buildings that exemplify this Orientalist bias. This type of evaluation, which has been widely criticised, is at odds with the evaluations of those within the architectural practice of these countries. Thus, there are no viable grounds for claiming that Western evaluation is more valid than an evaluation from within a particular historical architectural tradition.

After the collapse of the Ottoman Empire and the nationalist War of Liberation, Turkey embarked on building a nation-state. It adopted a modernising principle that might be described as 'Westernisation despite the West'. The statesmen of this new era saw the West as a source of both good and evil. The West was evil because it was considered to obstruct Turkey's modernisation, which the West saw as a threat to its own interests. Nevertheless, Turkey persevered in implementing a radical project of modernisation across all social spheres, marked by its significant attention to architecture.

At the time the Turkish Republic was founded, a neoclassical architecture referring to the Ottoman and Seljuk architectures that had preceded it, and described as 'nationalist' predominated. The founders of the new republic rejected this style of architecture because they sought to found their nationalism on recognition within an international context. This meant that instead of an architecture that referred to the past, Turkish architects were expected to work within a contemporary idiom and produce work that was on a par with the work of Western architects.

Turgut Cansever, Nautical Archaeological Institute, Bodrum, 1992–8
Opposite
The use of repetitive local architectural elements constructed with artisanal sensitivity is a fresh interpretation of regionalism.

Cengiz Bektas, Olbia Social Centre, Antalya, 1999
Right
The detached social units of a Modernist university are linked alongside a series of open spaces, invoking the spirit of an Oriental bazaar.

When Turkey embraced this ambitious objective, it did not actually possess a sufficient number of architects trained along contemporary lines. In Ankara, the new capital of Turkey, many new buildings were required. In order to meet this demand, a small number of foreign Modernist architects were invited to the country, and educational institutions were reorganised to provide training in the new idiom. Though various foreign architects designed buildings during this period, care was taken not to turn Turkey into a commercial arena. The Great Depression of 1929 sharpened sensitivity on this subject and, whilst official campaigns encouraged the public to buy local goods, international architectural competitions were held in order to put pressure on Turkish architects to raise the level of their work. The international competition held for the design of the Local Products and Savings Society building was won by a Turkish architect, Sevki Balmumcu, demonstrating that Turkish architects were capable of competing on an international level. It was realised that competitions had an important function in protecting the domestic market.

During the 1930s, architectural and engineering practices, and building development, in Turkey were institutionalised along lines of Modernist legitimacy. However, the number of trained architects was insufficient to meet all construction demands. During these years, Turkey began training a new generation of architects with the help of prominent German academics who had been compelled to flee from Germany.

Following the Second World War, Turkey experienced rapid urbanisation. Adapting to this radical transformation demanded both rapid industrialisation and urban building development at a time when Turkey, in only the early stages of its economic development, did not have the necessary level of capital accumulation. Moreover, the new arrivals in the cities did not have the cultural and financial capacity to meet the demands of institutionalised modernity. Under these circumstances, the new arrivals sought solutions to their own problems in accordance with their own rural traditions, with the result that cities became surrounded by shanty-town belts.

In the wake of the Second World War, architectural practice was limited to two spheres. The first was prestigious public buildings, and the second the 'build and sell' sector that developed spontaneously as a means of meeting the housing demands of the middle classes. Turkish architects rapidly embraced the international architectural idiom and developed an architectural philosophy that distanced itself from the inward-looking strategies that had been aimed at protecting the domestic architectural market.

The outcome of this approach was in line with the republic's modernising principles. The construction of prestigious new buildings was therefore governed by architectural competitions, which made it easier for young architects to obtain commissions and speeded up the transformation of architectural concepts. Success in competitions began to determine the level of prestige architects enjoyed. Studies in the field of the history of architecture are largely confined to this aspect. Architects who did not participate in competitions either followed the Modernist school within state bureaucracy or made a living designing 'build and sell' apartment buildings, and were excluded from academic architectural evaluations.

These internal dynamics continued into the 1980s. Significant changes came with the emergence of globalisation when Modernist

Success in competitions began to determine the level of prestige architects enjoyed. Studies in the field of the history of architecture are largely confined to this aspect. Architects who did not participate in competitions either followed the Modernist school within state bureaucracy or made a living designing 'build and sell' apartment buildings, and were excluded from academic architectural evaluations.

thought faced serious criticism. At this important time, although Turkish architects occasionally produced Postmodernist designs, this tactic was no longer effective in protecting the domestic market. The Turkish economy was opening up to the outside world, and altering its strategy in favour of export-driven industrialisation. In such an environment it was no longer possible to defend protectionism in architecture, and thus the system by which architects obtained commissions changed radically. The state ceased to be an attractive employer and was replaced by the private sector; impartial project distribution by means of state-sector competitions no longer defined the degree of prestige enjoyed by architects.

During this period, the number of architectural schools in Turkey had risen to 30, and the number of architects exceeded 30,000. Around 10 high-quality

Behruz Çinici, Turkish Grand National Assembly Mosque, Ankara, 1989
Opposite, top right
Rejecting all possible past and present traditional elements, Çinici creates a sacred and secular space for a secular parliament.

Tuncay Çavdar, Cappadocia Lodge Hotel, Urgup, 1990
Opposite, bottom right
Çavdar created an architecture that is integrated with its surroundings, inspired by the fascinating topography of Cappadocia.

Doğan Tekeli, Halk Bankasi headquarters, Ankara, 1993–8
Opposite, left
Suspended loggia-gardens placed in the carved volume of the mass create a human touch.

Murat Tabanlıoğlu, Doğan Group Printing Works, Ankara, 1995
Below left and right
Tabanlıoğlu used permanent values of Modernism, like functionalism, to guide his design.

Gökhan Avcioğlu, Philippe Robert and Haluk Sezgin, Adaptive re-use of 200-year-old Esma Sultan Waterfront House, Istanbul, 1999
Top and bottom
A glass box with a frameless suspended glass system is constructed inside the remaining historical walls in order to prevent the new intervention from overshadowing the old building.

The story of the development of Modernist architectural practice in Turkey … is marked both by failures and achievements. However, one significant aspect validates the whole story: while remaining in contact with the outside world, and without rejecting the phenomenal architectural values that evolved within Turkey itself, architecture in Turkey continues to compete with the outside world.

architectural journals were being published, giving architecture an influential public voice. The success of architects in Turkey was now determined by coverage of their buildings in these journals. This is a distinctive aspect of Turkish architecture, one that is rare among both developing and developed countries. Turkey had discovered a way of creating a system of values and a means of grading recognition within the broader architectural community.

This, briefly, is the story of the development of Modernist architectural practice in Turkey. It is marked both by failures and achievements. However, one significant aspect validates the whole story: while remaining in contact with the outside world, and without rejecting the phenomenal architectural values that evolved within Turkey itself, Turkish architecture continues to compete with the outside world.

A large number of studies have been published by Turkish historians of architecture – particularly since 1973, the 50th anniversary of the republic – about the achievements of contemporary Turkish architecture. Television's cultural channels have broadcast programmes about the major works of modern Turkish architects, and since 1988 the Turkish Chamber of Architects has been holding national architecture exhibitions every two years, and awarding prizes to architects/buildings selected by juries. Since 1980, Turkish architects have also achieved a notable degree of success in the Aga Khan architectural awards, which are held every three years, and outstanding buildings by Turkish architects have been published in various monographs and collections.

As a result, 10 or so architects have been recognised as pioneers of Modern architecture in Turkey since the 1950s. Among these, not one has sought a direct relationship with the Ottoman architecture of the past or deployed the grammar of Islamic architecture per se. All have made use of modern international technology, and employed a rational Western architectural language that reflects the ideology of the Turkish Republic. At the same time, they have endeavoured to create an architectural idiom unique to Turkey, which ranges from abstract international interpretation to a synthesis of national and universal characteristics.

Sedat Hakki Eldem (1908–88) who, for around 50 years, was a leading figure of Turkish architecture – as teacher, researcher and practising architect – interpreted traditional Turkish vernacular architecture with new materials and technology in his attempt to create a modern Turkish architectural language. Several of his waterfront houses (yalis) on the Bosporus, his Istanbul Law Courts, banks and consular buildings are very successful designs, their architecture based on a reinterpretation of the traditional Turkish house, with particular facade proportions and refined details. However, Eldem's architecture may be criticised for its prioritisation of aesthetic considerations over functional requirements.

The Turkish Historical Institute's building in Ankara, designed by Turgut Cansever, a student of Eldem's and for a while his assistant, is acknowledged as one of the finest exponents of the architectural approach that reinterprets the traditional without forming direct relations with it.[2] In contrast to the authoritative attitude of the architect in the Western world, Cansever maintains that the role of the architect is that of guide, architecture being a spontaneous building process in which the architect is only one of many components.[3] With this approach, he creates an open-ended architecture, which gives the impression of having formed of its own accord and being capable of evolving and extending. His Demir Holiday Resort in Bodrum, which won the Aga Khan architecture prize in 1992, is one of the best examples of this approach. And the building of the Nautical Archaeological Institute in Bodrum takes shape in accordance with Cansever's proposal to create an alternative form of production to modernity, as in the Arts and Crafts movement. The architect explains that here he has endeavoured to create a sense of open-ended, infinite space in all possible directions, including the sky.[4]

Cengiz Bektas, who seeks the anonymity of folk architecture in his designs,[5] displays a different

approach. He might be called a modern rationalist. He completes his designs based on clear geometrical lines defined by function, complementing them with skilfully arranged facades.[6] What he wished to say in the Kangotan House in Datça and the Sümer Pek House in Ann Arbor is that modern Turkish architecture, from within its contemporary identity, is obliged to reconcile its culture with the constantly evolving world. In his design for the Olbia Social Centre in Antalya, which won the Aga Khan prize in 2001, he displayed an abstract, anonymous approach to forms of vernacular construction, and in reference to the traditional Oriental bazaar linked the detached social units of a Modernist university layout by a street consisting of human-scale spaces.

With his unique, highly sensitive and spontaneous approach to design, Behruz Çinici occupies a distinctive place in modern Turkish architecture.[7] He is widely renowned for his design for the Middle East Technical University campus, in Ankara, and numerous original buildings, particularly the architectural faculty, on this campus. In all of these buildings, and in his later designs, he does not make any local or international references. Since there is no question of predetermined restrictive conditions, design is an instinctive experimental process. The most interesting and well-known example of this approach is his Turkish Grand National Assembly Mosque. Rejecting all past and present traditional elements associated with the mosque, Çinici exhibits a firm departure from the mosque concept. He explains: 'This is a building of faith, but commissioned and built by a secular state. And its essence describes liberty, democracy and equality; all the aspects on which our state is built.'[8]

Konuralp is an architect who follows the universal course of Modernism and, as he has pointed out, there is a duality in his designs: 'Apart from vernacular architecture, references to our cultural heritage, especially in circumstances demanding very advanced technology that essentially dictates its own morphology, cannot go beyond mannerism or an architectural caprice.'[9] The steel and glass building incorporating both printing facilities and offices, which he designed for *Sabah* newspaper, is entirely Western in conception and uses advanced technology. In contrast, in designing his Sagra House and Guesthouse in Ordu, and a residence in Dragos, Istanbul, he has sought a contemporary interpretation of the traditional.

Another representative of international architecture in Turkey is Sevki Vanli, whose designs exclude traditional elements, both in the formal and spatial sense. Vanli frankly admits that he is not a functionalist.[10] He displays a deductive, formal attitude, which embraces the doctrines of classical Modernism in an organic framework: 'I experience design as envisaging a building in an entirely finished image,' he says.[11]

Doğan Tekeli and Sami Sisa represent a milestone in the history of Turkish architecture with their awareness of institutionalisation rooted in rationality.[12] They describe their design process as induction that enables form to come into being as a result of its functional attributes.[13] They have treated industrial buildings within the framework of determining factors laid down by the industry for which they are designing, and with respect for the human requirements of the users. Their Lassa factory attracted international attention,[14] with its curved edges, human-scale windows, and vertical recesses and projections. Despite the building's huge dimensions in a surrounding that provides no reference, the architecture is on a humanly comprehensible scale. In the high-rise buildings the pair have designed recently, the references to the scale of the building have been treated as important elements. Two high-rise buildings in Ankara, designed for Halk Bankasi at a 10-year interval, have open, suspended gardens set within the mass of the building, lending scale and a human touch, as well as the requested symbolism.[15]

Tuncay Çavdar, another architect of this generation, exhibits a different approach, with his diversified architectural language. His architecture may be defined as a 'visual festival' and summarised as a search for formal diversity. His approach appears to be a disciplined Mannerism. At Pamfilya Holiday Resort he combines illusionary techniques with elements of Ottoman miniature painting;[16] while at Cappadocia Lodge Hotel he has created an architecture that is integrated with its setting, inspired by the fascinating topography of Cappadocia and an interpretation of it.

After the 1980s, this older generation of architects were joined by a new generation. Partly under the influence of globalisation, this differed from the earlier generation in aiming for a more universal architecture with greater self-confidence, feeling no compulsion to seek a synthesis of international and local. New employers representing Turkey's increasing capital accumulation support the design trends of this new generation. Almost all of these architects aim at breaking out of the narrow confines of Turkey to forge a dialogue with the world, using the discourse and technology of the West.[17]

Among them, Sevki Pekin stays distant from high technology, with a refined, Minimalist architecture that uses universal language. Han Tümertekin says that he begins by erasing all

that he knows, designing in a simple, universal language of architecture that he believes will enable him to achieve originality. Murat Tabanlioğlu's Doğan Group Printing Works is a major example of the use of permanent values of Modernism, like functionality, to guide his design and achieve an appropriate and clear expression of modern technology. Gökhan Avcioğlu works with a technology-centred, simple and transparent approach, which also has its counterparts in the Western world. His design (along with Philippe Robert and Haluk Sezgin) for the 200-year-old Esma Sultan Waterfront House is an example of this approach. In placing a glass box within the building, of which only the outer walls remain, he has made use of all of the opportunities offered by modern building technology. In this way an optical illusion is created that prevents the new building from overshadowing the historical.

Semra and Özcan Uygur are a young couple working from Ankara who in recent years have attracted attention with their prize-winning competition designs for large public buildings. Their major educational complex for the TED Foundation's Ankara College reflects the qualities summarised above. Other prominent names of this generation include Nevzat Sayin, Emre Arolat, Can Çinici and Boran Ekinci.

And in addition to the above recounted group of architects, newer names and newer generations, strongly in touch with the new trends in the world, are now emerging.

It seems that, while attempting to preserve its own values, Turkish architecture, today, appears to have approached its goal of becoming an integral part of the architecture of the contemporary world. △

Notes
1 U Tanyeli, 'Recent Turkish architecture: a crisis of happiness', Space Design, no 346, July 1993, p 51.
2 D Kuban, 'A survey of modern Turkish architecture', Architecture in Continuity, Building in the Islamic World Today, Islamic Publications Ltd/Aperture (New York), 1985, p 70.
3 Tanyeli, op cit, p 52.
4 T Cansever, 'Institute of Nautical Archaeology Headquarters', A+U Architecture and Urbanism, 2000/7, no 358, p 20.
5 U Tanyeli, 'Cengiz Bektas ile Söylesi', Cengiz Bektas, Boyut Yayin (Istanbul), 2001, pp 25, 43.
6 C Bektas, Cengiz Bektas Mimarlik Çalismalari, Yaprak Kitabevi (Ankara), 1979, p 7; U Tanyeli, 'Cengiz Bektas ve Yeni Atatürkçü Düsünce', Cengiz Bektas, Boyut Yayin (Istanbul), 2001, p 43; D Kuban, op cit, p 72.
7 U Tanyeli, 'Behruz Çinici', Behruz Çinici, Boyut Yayin (Istanbul), 2001, p 8.
8 K Shulman, 'Lowering the veil', Metropolis, November 2003, p 140.
9 'Atilla Yücel, Mehmet Konuralp ile Söylesiyor', Arredamento Dekorasyon, no 31, November 1991, p 94.
10 S Vanli, Sevki Vanli Mimarlik Çalismalari, Yaprak Kitabevi (Ankara) 1977, p 10.
11 D Kuban, 'Vanli Üzerine', Arredamento Dekorasyon, no 33, January 1992, p 82.
12 U Tanyeli, 'Doğan Tekeli-Sami Sisa: Bir Kurumlasma Öyküsü', Doğan Tekeli-Sami Sisa, Boyut Yayin (Istanbul), 2001, p 17.
13 S Özkan, 'Mimarliğa Adanmis Kirk Yil', Doğan Tekeli-Sami Sisa, Boyut Yayin (Istanbul), 2001, p 81.
14 Ibid, pp 83–4.
15 A Yücel, 'Doğan Tekeli-Sami Sisa Ile Konusma', Doğan Tekeli-Sami Sisa, Boyut Yayin (Istanbul), 2001, p 44.
16 U Tanyeli, op cit, p 52.
17 Ibid.

Semra and Özcan Uygur, Educational complex for the TED Foundation's Ankara College, Ankara, 1998
Opposite, top and bottom
The Uygurs' design reflects the ideas of the new generation which uses universal language and modern technology.

WORLD, OPEN CITY?

Does globalisation really dissolve borders and facilitate a free flow of capital, enabling the onset of a new unbiased era of multicapitalism? Esra Akcan looks below the surface at the prevailing distribution of power. She asks if Islamic countries are coming to represent a new 'other', as in the wake of 9/11 Islam becomes a new metonym for the 'non-Western'.

WORLD = CITY. The back cover of *Mutations*, by Rem Koolhaas, Stefano Boeri, Sanford Kwinter, Nadia Tazi and Hans Ulrich Obrist, provides a straightforward short cut to the impact of globalisation on architectural knowledge.[1] WORLD = CITY implies not only that the world is increasingly becoming urbanised, but also that globalisation is turning it into an intertwined set of urban zones. In current discussions, the city has replaced the village as a metaphor to describe the contemporary pace of communications and capital flows across the globe. The crucial question here is whether this city is fortified or open, medieval or modern, in conception.

Socioeconomic theories of globalisation usually focus on the decreasing authority of national borders in determining the flow of capital during the era of multinational capitalism.[2] Information highways also point in the same direction, emphasising the openness of, and connectivity between, the zones. However, our contemporary world seems as an open city only to those who ignore the prevailing geographical distribution of power. There is actually no smooth correspondence between the flow of information and capital, and the flow of people.

A quick look at the visa application rooms of today is enough to confirm this point – those architecturally neglected yet indicative spaces which exemplify a unique combination of panoptic and heterotopic spatial principles, where a group of racially and ethnically mixed immigrants ('usual suspects') wait for hours under the disciplinary gaze of officials. The ideologies of Orientalism, colonialism and

'Eurocolonies' map by Rem Koolhaas/AMO/OMA
Opposite
The Eurocolonies map appeared in Rem Koolhaas' report "Brussels: Capital of Europe," submitted in October 2001. The colours representing the countries in Europe match the ones used for their ex-colonies.
Even though many architects may have been conscious about Eurocentrism and the violent history of colonisation before this representation, this map evidently revealed to the discipline the extent of Western hegemony throughout the world during the colonial periods.

Turgut Cansever, Demir Housing Complex, Bodrum, 1983 (starting date)
Above right
In his work, especially during the late 1980s and early 1990s in Turkey, Turgut Cansever referred to Islam as a guide for his architectural approach. Nevertheless, his design practice is not based on stereotypical iconographic symbols of Islamic architecture. This provides yet another example for the conceptual fragility of the term 'Islamic architecture', especially for the modern period, as a generalising art-historical category.

In current discussions, the city has replaced the village as a metaphor to describe the contemporary pace of communications and capital flows across the globe. The crucial question here is whether this city is fortified or open, medieval or modern, in conception.

Eurocentrism do not appear to have disappeared just because capital can now flow with little friction between nation-states, and just because the Internet has been invented. While the world's borders are evaporating for some who can effortlessly travel from one continent to the other, and perform simultaneously in multiple zones, the same borders are becoming more and more closed for others. It is these 'others', usually referred to as 'non-Westerners', who this article addresses, not to maintain the category of 'otherness', but rather to criticise the very making of the 'other' in the first place.

Financial analyses of globalisation remind us how the geography of centrality is increasingly being altered.[3] The word 'centre' no longer simply connotes New York, London, Paris, but rather a virtual network, an electronic highway that connects various global cities that can potentially be located at any place around the globe, including Tokyo, Hong Kong, Mumbai and São Paulo. At least some of the 'other' geographies of the 'West' are now crucial for the global market to sustain itself. Today, it is by placing a child from Africa in the advertisement, asking 'Are you ready?' behind the white screen, that Internet companies try to convince us of their revolution in communication technologies. For the inhabitants of the zones that were hitherto noncentral,

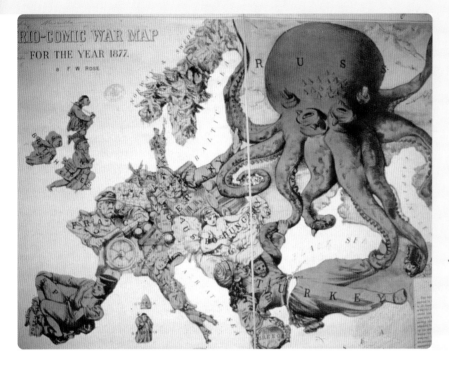

The architects in these countries are justified in their simultaneous excitement and anxiety over globalisation. On the one hand, globalisation opens up new possibilities of employment and collaboration, and creates excitement about being connected to the centre; on the other, competition in the job market at the global level leads to anxiety about losing areas of production that once belonged to local professionals.

'Serio-Comic War Map, for the Year 1877', by Frederick Rose (in John Goss, *Mapmaker's Art*)
Above
Map-making is a graphic practice commonly used to illustrate and simultaneously construct political representations of the world by mapmakers and architects alike.

'The World of Civilizations', map from Samuel Huntington's *Clash of Civilizations*
Opposite
In *Clash of Civilizations and the Remaking of World Order*, Huntington argued that in the post-Cold War period the main political tensions were cultural, and visualised his argument in this atlas. dividing the world into a series of civilisations. 'Clash of civilisations' became a catchword, especially in conservative circles, in public discussions after 9/11, constructing an image of Islamic countries as being essentially incommensurable with the West – its 'civilisational other', and an extreme and unbridgeable enemy.

however, globalisation creates complex and contradictory feelings.

The architects in these countries are justified in their simultaneous excitement and anxiety over globalisation. On the one hand, globalisation opens up new possibilities of employment and collaboration, and creates excitement about being connected to the centre; on the other, competition in the job market at the global level leads to anxiety about losing areas of production that once belonged to local professionals.

Theories that privilege economic processes alone fall short in explaining all the forces of globalisation that transform architecture. If the world aspires to connect beyond the virtual and economic level, many questions remain unresolved: Is (Will) globalisation (be) imitative of the imperialist attitude, or is it possible to turn the forces of globalisation towards a more fruitful and democratic dialogue between different places of the world? Does globalisation bring a paradigm shift in the transportation of architectural knowledge and services, or does it only accelerate the historic processes? Namely, are we talking about a unidirectional cultural flow, almost exclusively from the European and North American world to their 'others', or a dialogical cultural encounter?

Can/should we assume to have gone beyond the tired dichotomies of West versus East, when separatist terms such as 'clash of civilisations' continue to texture reflections on the

contemporary world put forth by even the most 'critical' architects? How inspiring can a transnational building practice be, if world architects remain uninformed and unprepared for such a task because of their insufficient historical knowledge and theoretical sophistication on the architecture of 'non-Western' countries?

Consider the undertones of the term 'Islamic countries'. What does Islam connote today in relation to architecture? This term has already been subject to multiple misconceptions, basically because of the constructed category of 'Islamic architecture'. Used since the 19th century to emphasise its radical difference from the artistic experience of the Western world, 'Islamic art and architecture' had been expected to cover an extensive scope from 8th-century Spain to modern India. However, as recent historians in the field have also emphasised, an overarching art-historical category for such a broad scope is untenable. Islam itself is by no means a universally homogenous religion, since its practice in different countries around the world can hardly be generalised. 'Islam' is a term that effects an extremely broad geographical range, from the US to Iraq, whether the groups that are associated with it are a minority or a majority, vocally disinterested in the place of this religion in their lives or its passionate proponents.

'Islamic architecture' as an art-historical term misleadingly categorises a whole body of architectural practice in countries associated with Islam as religious. However, the architectural legacies of each of these countries stretch back well before Islam began to have an effect on their built environments; and even when this occurred, the emerging architecture was informed by what already existed, and guided by nonreligious concerns. The explanatory limits of a term such as Islamic architecture are no less than with, say, 'Christian architecture' or 'Jewish architecture', and using the first more frequently than the latter two is inconsistent epistemologically, and conservative ideologically. Islam, or any religion, should not be a category with which we fix an opinion on architecture.

This is not to deny that there have been some modern architects who have stated that they want to establish their own architectural principles based on Islam. Usually motivated by a critique of modernisation for corrupting, polluting or destroying what they defend as Islamic culture before a Western-oriented modernisation, there have been architects who have referred to Islam as a guide for their architectural practice. But even in these cases, for example Turgut Cansever in his work during the late 1980s and early 1990s in Turkey,[4] the design practice is not based on stereotypical iconographic symbols of 'Islamic architecture', such as domes, arches or minarets, but rather in a way that is more complex, subtle and layered.

'Islamic architecture' has hardly any explanatory power especially for the modern design practice, and recently a new, much more worrying, phase is being added to this history. Islam is rapidly turning into a social category of exclusion. In mainstream political representations, the term 'Islamic countries' is beginning to connote the 'others' of the 'Western' self. Geographical categorisations, which are then used as premises of exclusion, have historically been very common in architectural knowledge. Architectural history is still written and taught in schools by employing tired categories such as the 'Western' and the 'non-Western'. It seems that a geographical 'other' – the 'non-West' – is sharply inscribed in our imaginations, which in turn influences pedagogical, disciplinary and professional concerns, not only in European and North American countries, but also in countries that fall into the category of the 'non-West'.[5]

However, 'non-West' not only refers to and maintains the ideology of an exaggerated difference between the West and its others, but also disavows the differences within these others. It completely undermines the centuries-long hybridisations between these geographical zones – their intertwined histories, their effects on the cultural imaginations of each other – as if a 'pure West' and a 'pure East' can exist. Today, maintaining the imaginary border between the West and its geographical

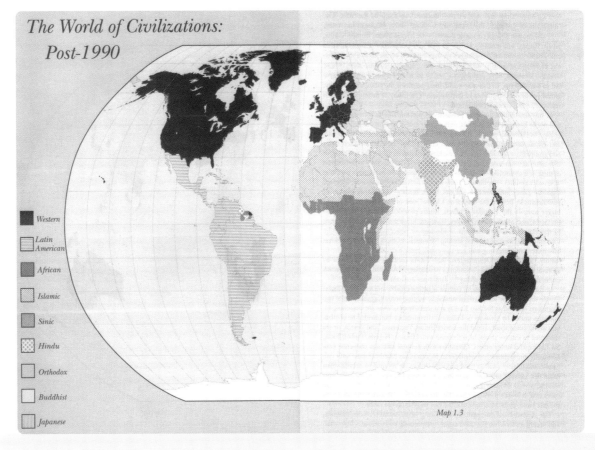

The World of Civilizations:
Post-1990

Western

Latin American

African

Islamic

Sinic

Hindu

Orthodox

Buddhist

Japanese

Map 1.3

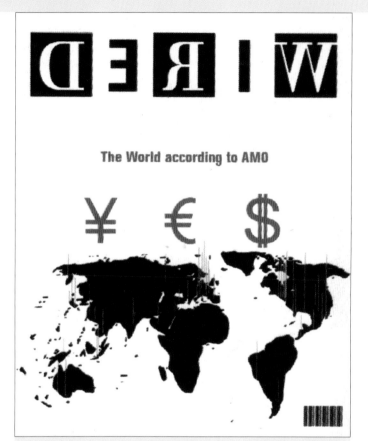

The World according to AMO

¥ € $

Recent responses to globalisation are changing the content of this geographical divide, while maintaining its basic ideological premises. A number of geographical zones that were previously considered 'non-Western' are now being included as subjects of globalisation, whereas Islamic countries as a whole are increasingly seen as a threat to globalisation. While the otherness of some countries in east and Southeast Asia are now being erased, the so-called Islamic countries are being defined as globalisation's other.

other can hardly create any critical strategy in responding fruitfully to current political conflicts.

Recent responses to globalisation are changing the content of this geographical divide, while maintaining its basic ideological premises. A number of geographical zones that were previously considered 'non-Western' are now being included as subjects of globalisation, whereas Islamic countries as a whole are increasingly seen as a threat to globalisation. While the otherness of some countries in east and Southeast Asia is now being erased, the so-called Islamic countries are being defined as globalisation's other. In summary, all of the epistemological and ethical problems surrounding the term 'non-Western' are now being allocated to what are called the Islamic countries. Islam is becoming the new metonym for the 'non-Western'.

The dominant forces of globalisation are redrawing the atlas of the world, and yet they are not undoing the imaginary border between the West and its other, intensifying the emphasis on some zones. Thinking about Islam and architecture today is thus a crucial topic, not because Islam should become a fixed category in architectural criticism, but because the subject reveals the ideological borders surfacing in reflections about globalisation itself; its self-definition and inclusions, as well as its exclusions and ways of maintaining hierarchies.

Again, this is not to deny that there are simultaneous movements carried by groups who base their principles on Islam. Whether these are movements that may be described as other-globalisation (trying to unite nations under Islam) or anti-globalisation, they should not be categorically confused with the term Islamic countries used as a generalising term, which is then employed for the sake of exclusion. That is, the conflation of globalisation's other with other-globalisation or anti-globalisation as interchangeable categories is a problem, not to mention the confusion of any of these with political terrorism.

Take 'clash of civilisations' for instance, which has become a catchword in public discussions post-9/11. The term had already been famously used in an article by Bernard Lewis in 1990, who asked: Now that France has left Algeria and Britain has left Egypt – that is, now that colonisation is no more – why do Muslims still resent 'us', and concluded: 'Clearly something deeper is involved than these specific grievances, numerous and important as they may be – something deeper that turns every disagreement into a problem and makes every problem insoluble.'[6] It was this 'deeper something' that Lewis termed a 'clash of civilisations'.[7]

The term reappeared in 1996, much more prominently as the title of Samuel P Huntington's book *The Clash of Civilizations and the Remaking of World Order*. 'We know who we are only when we know who we are not and often when we know whom we are against,'[8] began Huntington, illustrating his argument with a series of atlases speaking to the changing picture of world politics in the 20th century. This is a graphic practice that has been commonly used to illustrate and simultaneously construct political representations of the world, not only by map-makers but also by architects such as Buckminster Fuller and Rem Koolhaas.

Huntington's first atlas, entitled *The West and the Rest – 1920*, unapologetically illustrated the Western hegemony throughout the world as a result of colonisation. (Rem Koolhaas' map 'Eurocolonies'' is a very similar multicolour version of this atlas, though not necessarily with similar intentions.) His second atlas, illustrating the Cold War, divided the world into the 'free world' and the 'communist bloc', and added the category of 'unaligned nations'. But in the post-Cold War period, Huntington argued, the main political tensions were cultural, and the world was divided into a series of civilisations that were mostly, though not exclusively, categorised in relation to religions. 'Islamic civilisation' was one of the nine in Huntington's list,[9] a category that included the Middle East, North Africa and some parts of central and Southeast Asia. Yet still, the 'central distinction', he wrote, 'is between the West as the hitherto dominant civilization and all the others which, however, have little if anything in common among them. The world, in short, is divided between a Western one and a non-Western many.'[10]

In the post-9/11 world, it was just one more step to deem Islamic countries among this 'non-Western many' as the 'civilisational other' of the West, its extreme and unbridgeable enemy. Ignoring all the historic constituencies of the rise of political Islam in the late- and post-Cold War era,[11] in public discussions the 'clash of civilisations' became the popular explanation of world events, constructing an image of Islamic countries as something essentially and timelessly incommensurable with the West. As if a 'pure West' and a 'pure East' could exist; as if there could ever be a self-contained history to Western civilisation, this argument ignored centuries of intertwined histories, connections and influences across different parts of the world.

However unintentional they may be, current architectural reflections on globalisation, by vocal and influential architects, run the risk of maintaining the ideological constructs of this talk of a 'clash of civilisations'. For example, the implications of the term resurfaced during many

of the discussions surrounding the new World Trade Center competition in New York. Daniel Libeskind explained his project as an 'icon that speaks of our vitality in the face of danger'.[12] He defined the remaining slurry walls surrounding his sunken plaza as the symbol of the West's founding principles that survived the attack. The wound had to manifest itself physically in the site by this cut because, the architect declared, the attack was not a 'historical and past memory that is over, but an ongoing one' and thus the architecture of the whole site had to serve as a reminder of 'the attack against the foundations on which we stand'.[13]

These words resonated in tune with the 'clash of civilisations' argument, even if I can hardly imagine that this was Libeskind's intention. Yet, for many, the competition project thus represented permanent danger, revenge and continuing hostility, and not aspirations towards 'perpetual peace' or a humanist vision that could construct an inclusive vision of human possibility. Cosmopolitan law and hospitality were the two basic precepts for perpetual peace in Immanuel Kant's founding text,[14] but what happened during the public discussions about the World Trade Center site represented a paradoxical notion of cosmopolitanism for New York: an understanding of limited cosmopolitanism that cherishes the mixture of racial, ethnic and religious groups, and the coexistence of different languages being spoken in the global city, while maintaining assumptions about the persistence of essentially 'evil nations' living in a distant land.

Asia no longer connotes a 'non-Western other' in current architectural representations. Select countries less in conflict with Europe and North America are included in the fascinated remarks about the big, fast-growing, charmingly unorganised Asian cities, and yet others, from the same continent, are erased from such representations. While Japan has long been considered 'Western', China has recently become the new stage for the star architects. Rem Koolhaas and AMO/OMA's (Office of Metropolitan Architecture's) 'Regime of the ¥ £ $' (1999) was one of the earliest and most influential representations of this concept. This world picture promoted the seeming alliance and hidden competition of three world powers within the rules of Western capitalism. It was hospitable in including a 'non-Western' other, but seemed to do so only as long as this other was incorporated within the rules of the Western self (capitalism). The question concerning the intensifying poverty and otherness of the excluded zones remained unreflected.

Conversely, 'Go East' is the reiterated slogan of Koolhaas' recent book *Content* (2004), as 'a response to 9/11 mounting wreckage and an acknowledgment of the eastward momentum'.[15] Politically conscious and

'Regime of the ¥ £ $', map by Rem Koolhaas/AMO/OMA
Opposite
Asia no longer connotes a 'non-Western other' in current architectural representations. Rem Koolhaas' and AMO/OMA's 'Regime of the ¥ £ $' was a world picture that promoted the alliance and hidden competition of three world powers within the rules of Western capitalism. The question concerning the intensifying poverty and otherness of the excluded zones remained unreflected.

visionary positions fill the pages of this book, which escapes didacticism and, at first sight, looks like the work of an *enfant terrible.* Yet it includes articles (from AMO and outside) with strong ethical concerns critically questioning colonisation and current political conflicts in various parts of the world.

Koolhaas' call, in a deliberately childlike passage, for 'a new inclusive framework that could eventually accommodate every nation belonging to this landmass into a Judeochristian-Islamic-Hindu-Confusian belt of compatibility'[16] is certainly a much more productive and visionary position than the 'clash of civilisations' talk. However, one reservation still needs to be stated: an assumption of compatibility under a framework defined by a dominant power runs the risk of mimicking the age-old universalising attempts that ended in nothing but the colonialist extension of one's own system of reference to the other. If this becomes the case, it would only repeat the conventional dominant paradigm, namely the unidirectional and forced flow between places, rather than a dialogical interaction.

Recent architectural research into the growing global cities that do not limit themselves merely to the Western world are admirable, yet this alone can hardly be a value in itself, since history is saturated with architects and artists who were interested in the East and sought to represent it. Among these were many whose Orientalist representations (in Edward Said's sense)[17] produced the image of the Islamic and the Oriental as an inferior race that needed Western redemption and progress. However, there were also those who claimed to have found the 'universal' law of architecture based on the perceived compatibility of the 'non-Western' with their own principles.[18]

To give an example, in his book *Grammar of Ornament* Owen Jones declared that Islamic ornamentation was produced by the rational and geometrical ordering of flat surfaces, and that its use of colour was also scientific, and claimed that he found the universal law of ornament to be based on the rational treatment of nature.[19] In doing so, Jones assimilated Islamic ornamentation within his own frames of reference, and sought to make it a legitimising ground to prove the 'universality' of his own argument. Over a long history of Orientalist and Eurocentric knowledge about Islam and 'non-Western' architecture in general, it remains to be seen whether recent reflections on globalisation will manage to construct a paradigm shift.

In order to face and respond to the potential and challenges of globalisation, it is better to be guided by the human tradition (Western and 'non-Western') that emphasises and envisions unconditional hospitality, cosmopolitanism and intertwined histories, rather than the 'clash of civilisations' that assumes the existence of essential hostilities and differences between the peoples of the world. However, this can hardly be achieved by the extension of one's own language over other languages to make them the same as it; rather it can be achieved only by the expansion of languages to stimulate a more inclusive vision of humanity. ⌂

Notes
1 Rem Koolhaas, Stefano Boeri, Sanford Kwinter, Nadia Tazi and Hans U Obrist, *Mutations,* ACTAR (Barcelona), 2001.
2 In economic terms, globalisation is defined as the independence of the business market from national borders in late capitalism, which has been facilitated by advances in communications technologies. See Saskia Sassen, *Globalization and Its Discontents: Essays on the New Mobility of People and Money,* The New Press (New York), 1998; Saskia Sassen, 'The new centrality: the impact of telematics and globalization', in William S Saunders (ed), *Reflections on Architectural Practices in the Nineties,* Princeton Architectural Press (New York), 1996, pp 206–18; Manuel Castells, 'Globalization, flows and identity: the new challenges to design', in Saunders, op cit, pp 198–205; P Hall, 'Megacities, World Cities and Global Cities', lecture delivered in February 1997, www.megacities.nl.
3 Saskia Sassen, 'The new centrality', op cit.
4 Turgut Cansever, *Sehir ve Mimari,* Agaç Yayincilik (Istanbul), 1992; Turgut Cansever, *Ev ve Sehir,* Insan Yayinlari (Istanbul), 1994; Turgut Cansever, *Kubbeyi Yere Koymamak,* Iz Yayincilik (Istanbul), 1997.
5 Due to limited space, I can hardly expand this argument further in this article, but for my ideas and extended bibliography on the topic, see: Esra Akcan, 'Critical practice in the global era: question concerning "other" geographies', *Architectural Theory Review,* vol 7, no 1, 2002.
6 Bernard Lewis, 'The Roots of Muslim Rage', September 1990, www.theatlantic.com/issue/90sep/rage.htm. part 1, p 16.
7 'It should by now be clear that we are facing a mood and a movement far transcending the level of issues and policies and the governments that pursue them. This is no less than a clash of civilizations – the perhaps irrational but surely historic reaction of an ancient rival against our Judeo-Christian heritage, our secular present, and the worldwide expansion of both.' Ibid, part 2, p 14.
8 Samuel P Huntington, *The Clash of Civilizations and the Remaking of World Order,* Simon & Schuster (New York and London), 1996, p 21.
9 The categories were: Western, Latin American, African, Islamic, Sinic, Hindu, Orthodox, Buddhist and Japanese.
10 Huntington, op cit, p 36.
11 In his latest book, Mahmood Mamdani argues that: 'rather than illustrating a deep-seated clash of civilizations, 9/11 came out of recent history, that of the late Cold War.' Mahmood Mamdani, *Good Muslim, Bad Muslim,* Pantheon Books (New York), 2004, p 11.
12 Daniel Libeskind's explanation of his competition project (www.renewnyc.com). The same explanation was also distributed as a booklet during the exhibition: *Plans in Progress: Innovative Design Study for the World Trade Center Site,* LMDC, December 2002.
13 Q&A Forum on WTC Competition, 16 January 2003, New York.
14 My debt to contemporary reconsiderations of Kant's term and Kant's own text should be clear. Immanuel Kant, 'Perpetual peace: a philosophical sketch', in H Reiss and HB Nisbet (eds), *Political Writings,* Cambridge University Press (Cambridge), 1970, 1999..
15 AMO/OMA/Rem Koolhaas, Brendan McGetrick, Simon Brown and Jon Link, *Content,* Taschen (Cologne), 2004, p 16.
16 Ibid, p 388.
17 Edward Said, *Orientalism,* Vintage (New York), 1978, 1994.
18 For a discussion on related historical examples and theoretical texts, see Esra Akcan, op cit.
19 Owen Jones, *Grammar of Ornament,* Van Nostrand Reinhold (New York), 1992, original 1856.

Islam
and the Avant-Garde

Architecture in Islamic lands is more commonly associated with a nostalgic revival of a golden inheritance than the avant-garde. But an impressive number of innovative architects practising at an international level, have Middle Eastern backgrounds – one only has to think of Zaha Hadid, Farshid Moussavi of FOA, or Hani Rashid of Asymptote. **Jeremy Melvin** here explores the relationship between Islam and the avant-garde, and how a culture richly steeped in geometry, mathematics and fractals has been able to infuse architecture globally at the cutting edge.

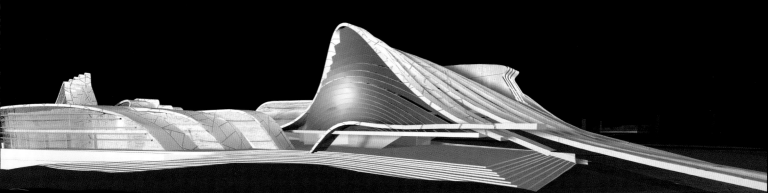

No aspect of history appeals more to the 'What if?' tendency than the relationship between Islam and the West. As the most distinguished Occidental scholar of the Islamic world, Bernard Lewis, pointed out, had the Ottomans achieved their realistic intention of conquering Italy at the dawn of the Renaissance the world would have developed in a very different way. If Charles Martel had lost at Poitiers in 732, would the Oxford Schools, asked that Big Daddy of historians, Edward Gibbon rhetorically, have been devoted to interpretations of the Koran? Thus posing the question of what might have happened if Hadid's Strasbourg Mosque had been built, could open fruitful territory for speculation.

At the very least it would have tested the possibility of whether the ritualistic needs of a mosque could be met by a design from the contemporary avant-garde. It would also have given Europe its most distinguished mosque since the Great Mosque of Cordoba. And, in this juxtaposition, it would have realigned Islam and the avant-garde, recalling that for centuries the most outward-looking, inventive and innovative cultural achievements on European soil or its immediate neighbours came from the Islamic world. These achievements underpinned Gothic architecture and its philosophical and theological counterpart, Scholasticism. Assisted by the greater scope and better techniques for trade that reached Europe from the Levant, they also helped to shape the Renaissance.

Professor Reinhard Schultze of Bern University's Institut für Islamwissenschaft & Neuere Orientalische Philologie puts a historical perspective on the term 'avant-garde'. In its current form it emerged as a political term in the mid-19th century, and only came to designate innovative art a generation or so later. Given the problematic relationship between Western and Islamic cultures, it is hardly surprising that the term resonated, rebounded and ricocheted in unpredictable ways as the concept of avant-garde began to shape cultural discourse in the Muslim world, just as it did in the West and Japan.

Professor Reinhard Schultze of Bern University's Institut für Islamwissenschaft & Neuere Orientalische Philologie puts a historic perspective on the term 'avant-garde'. In its current form it emerged as a political term in the mid-19th century, and only came to designate innovative art a generation or so later. Given the problematic relationship between Western and Islamic cultures, it is hardly surprising that the term resonated, rebounded and ricocheted in unpredictable ways as the concept of avant-garde began to shape cultural discourse in the Muslim world, just as it did in the West and Japan. Ottoman artists living in Paris during the late 19th century adopted the term in its Westernised sense, and thereby 'took part in Orientalist discourse'. But for intellectuals living across the Muslim world, the concept of the avant-garde echoed with the ancient Arabic term *tali'a*, originally used in a military context, which was picked up by Egyptian Fabians in the early 20th century and continued to be 'an elitist self description ... of very great importance in the Muslim world' throughout the century.

Suha Özkan, secretary-general of the Aga Khan Award for Architecture, explains these complex implications in the present day. Dubai Hotels may be avant-garde, but this is no guarantee of quality. Some Gulf countries, notably Qatar, have looked to the international avant-garde and commissioned work from Arata Isozaki, Calatrava and Jean Nouvel, who has a scheme for the Doha Corniche. Yet there are also architects, from Malaysia's Ken Yeang to Omrania and Zuhair Fayez, in Riyadh and Jeddah respectively, who are innovating within, and demonstrating some of the variations within, Islamic cultures.

Foreign Office Architects (FOA) cofounder Farshid Moussavi, who was born in Iran and educated in the UK and US, and who served on the jury of the recent Aga Khan awards, finds similar qualifications necessary. She distinguishes between Islamic architecture – primarily the design of mosques and associated religious buildings – and architecture in the Muslim world. Recent trends, she argues, have driven the first category towards symbolism and, hence, pastiche. Easily assimilated features like symmetry and conventional patterns are generally considered adequate conveyers of the religious message. In explaining her difficulty with this situation, she says: 'Symbolism reduces to image and excludes performance.' The 'particular typology' of the mosque, Moussavi feels, 'could be pushed interestingly', but it would 'take huge courage', demanding that Hadid-like duality of skills: iconoclasm and an ability to reconstruct the essence of what those icons might represent with imaginative sympathy and creativity.

For Moussavi, one of the first considerations would be to consider how programme might influence the form and, hence, experience and impression of a mosque. But this happens in few, if any, cases. Hanif Kara, whose firm Adams Kara Taylor has engineered some of Hadid's and FOA's most innovative structures, as well as others by Alsop and Foster, outlines one of the reasons, at least in the UK. Too many new mosques, he argues, are 'designed' by people from within the communities they serve, who are all too often technicians rather than architects. Without either the age or experience that would give them authority within their own social network, or the qualifications that might carry weight in a large constituency, it is easy for them to accept the expectations of their elders, and the Saudi Arabian sources who frequently give financial support. The result is pastiche tending towards parody.

The difference between this reality and the possibilities which Hadid's Strasbourg design opens up, recalls a critical episode in 19th-century Western architectural history. When Ruskin explained to his father that, though the 'outward test' of Gothic architecture was the pointed arch, its real essence lay in the state of mind of the workman, he made an extraordinary leap in perception. What really mattered was inner feeling, not outer form. This is but one episode in the enormous psychological trauma that faced Western society in the 19th century, as what had been taken for literal certainties were gradually revealed to have truth, if at all, in some metaphorical form. On such perceptions rests almost the entire subsequent history of art and much else besides. One of the consequences was a direct invitation to spurn artistic conventions, a condition that underpinned the *raison d'être* of the Modernist

From the vantage point of judging the Aga Khan's awards, Moussavi takes a broader and less dogmatic view. Architecture across the Muslim world offers more interesting scope than the problems surrounding mosque design. She takes a typically wide perspective: 'The Muslim world is full of different cultures … the Middle East has as much diversity as Europe … and there are as many different styles.'

avant-garde. Even with the necessary caution about transferring situations from one century and culture to another, it is tempting to see an analogy with Hadid's design, whose affinity with other mosques would have lain in the emotions it evoked rather than the images it presented.

While there is no reason why the tenets of Western Modernism should have a stranglehold over what is considered to be progressive, radical, innovative and creative – although all of these terms are loaded – to some such a barrier makes an insuperable distinction between architecture in the Islamic world and the avant-garde. Hani Rashid, the Egyptian-born, US-educated partner in the fashionable New York firm Asymptote, is quite happy to claim a place in the contemporary avant-garde, but denies any connection between his work and architecture in Muslim cultures.

From the vantage point of judging the Aga Khan's awards, Moussavi takes a broader and less dogmatic view. Architecture across the Muslim world offers more interesting scope than the problems surrounding mosque design. She takes a typically wide perspective: 'The Muslim world is full of different cultures … the Middle East has as much diversity as Europe … and there are as many different styles.' Its geographic size and climatic extremes – from Russian steppes to the tropics – ensure that nature has endowed it with different architectural traditions. Before acting as a judge, Moussavi had 'expected more root [among the entries] in identifiable cultural traditions', but instead saw compatibilities with architecture in the West: 'The same processes that generate architecture are present … [in many cases] similar technologies and the same daily issues.' With some examples she was left to 'wonder if they were Western or just contemporary buildings'. Where secular buildings strive for an 'Islamic' identity, the result is a kitsch Postmodernism, just as

Zaha Hadid, design for Strasbourg Mosque, France, 2000

Opening page
If built, Zaha Hadid's Strasbourg Mosque would have re-established a connection between Islamic culture and avant-garde architecture, a connection that existed right the way through the Middle Ages, in buildings such as the Great Mosque in Cordoba, and into the period known as the Renaissance, in the magnificent mosques designed by the great Ottoman architect Sinan.

Below
Hadid's design balanced the specifically Islamic need for a prayer axis with a particular direction, and the curvature of the river. Where the two geometries, curving and straight, meet, they fractalise and generate volume. Architecture, therefore, arises from the interaction between a specific location and an abstract cultural ideal, and this interaction takes place through mathematics.

Where secular buildings strive for an 'Islamic' identity, the result is a kitsch Postmodernism, just as when Western elephantine office blocks essay historical reference. And similarly, again, there are the discreetly elegant examples of modern design which call attention to themselves by quality rather than bombast. In this, 'Iran is not so different to Seoulor Athens'.

when Western elephantine office blocks essay historical reference. And similarly, again, there are the discreetly elegant examples of modern design which call attention to themselves by quality rather than bombast. In this, 'Iran is not so different to Seoul or Athens'.

In Iran, Moussavi says, there is a 'thirst for Modernism'. Architects like Hadi Mirmiran and Bahram Shirdel, who taught with Jeff Kipnis at the Architectural Association before returning, are showing signs of moving beyond the old condition of a Western-educated elite trying to superimpose their acquired cultural values. Some building types, she explains, are starting to ask the question she poses rhetorically: 'What is the identity of industrial buildings, schools or housing?' At their best they combine fitness for purpose with recognition of differences of climate and culture, just what an awards jury might look for in the West. Among

those that have found their way into the Aga Khan's awards are some subtle houses in Turkey, and a school in North Africa, where the arid climate allows space-frame-like roof structures of steel reinforcing bars, which might almost be a very distant descendant of ABK's Maidenhead Library.

Turkey, with its secular constitution and relatively high level of economic development, has both the means and inclination to engage in architectural experimentation. As Hanif Kara points out, it has the largest number of architects in the Islamic world, and the universities to train them. His own experience, though, is quite different. Born into a Sunni Muslim community that had left Gujarat in India for East Africa a generation or two earlier, his family found themselves refugees in the UK during the early 1970s. In common with many diasporic communities, he had to decide on his level of engagement with his new context. Maintaining 'cultural roots [which are] to do with an Asian [rather than Islamic] way of life', he also discovered engineering and 'loved Tony Hunt [the great British engineer for whom he worked] before the Aga Khan', referring to a recent decision to join the Ismaili community. Within its framework he has begun to find ways of bringing together his interests in advanced engineering with his Islamic heritage.

What appealed to Kara about the Ismaili branch of Islam is that it is the 'most contemporary' of the various groupings that make up the Islamic world, and the only one with a living imam who comes in a direct lineage from the prophet Mohammed. One of Islam's most telling differences from Christianity, argues Bernard Lewis, is that from its earliest origins it combined the role of state and religion: there was no conflict such as that between God and Caesar which, for millennia, has run through Western history. Yet the Ismailis have no ambitions to form a state and so, according to Kara, they naturally engage with their host and neighbouring cultures; 'they become what they are in each country.' Consequently, there is an inbuilt receptivity to different ideas and less dependence on literalism. Kara contrasts this condition with the resorts being developed in Dubai, whose architecture shows a desperate schizophrenia, torn between the expectations of the clientele it hopes to attract and expressing some form of traditional culture. The resulting architectural confusion has its counterpart in its social composition: Dubai is the Middle East's prostitution capital.

For Kara, design is a discipline that runs deeper and does not necessarily manifest itself in a literal way. The 'guiding principles of trying not to tell lies, to dig deeper to help others', have always been a greater influence than 'domes or Islamic rituals'. The realisation that there may be a more subtle connection between belief and the contemporary condition has struck him 'only recently', and in particular through geometry. 'Many Islamic geometries', such as those on the great Islamic buildings of the past, he explains, 'are linked to fractals'. He has a long-standing interest in fractal geometry, and to exploit its potential, Adams Kara Taylor has recently established a specialist unit. But the interest goes further. 'These complex shapes,' he advances, 'are connected to real maths and real science,' one of the essences of engineering as it is understood in the West. Some arch forms or tiling patterns, for example, display the characteristics of fractals, where complex forms come from self-similar basic shapes.

In traditional Islamic societies, Kara argues, there was an 'embedded knowledge of materials and maths', though often worked out intuitively and established by trial and error. This ingrained understanding helped to engender precisely the sort of engagement between programme and use on the one hand, and symbolism and cultural tradition on the other, that Farshid Moussavi considers so important. Kara cites a building in Yemen, virtually a perfect cube, which is 'proportioned well for its climate', as well as being 'an important political space and a space for prayer'. As such it is a token of the potential of architecture for 'sustainability, in the sense of holding a community together'. He expresses an interest in pursuing the sort of line pioneered by Hassan Fathy, where various different strands of tradition, of varying degrees of literalness, come together in a way that could be both Islamic and contemporary.

For Moussavi, too, geometry offers one possible point of connection between tradition and contemporary. 'It could have room to get into the symbolism and turn it into part of the process,' she says, and it has the inherent possibility of being able 'to resonate [with the past] without replicating it ... It is impossible not to be fascinated with that area of enquiry.' Given the degree of diversity, the simultaneous opening up of opportunities as others may close down, and the evident eagerness of at least parts of the Islamic world to engage in such speculative enquiry, questions about the degree of interaction between the avant-garde and Islam may not be counterfactual for much longer. As Suha Özkan concludes: 'It is potentially a playground for everyone.' ⌀

Zaha Hadid, design for Strasbourg Mosque, France, 2000

Opposite
The mosque itself, and the courtyard, float above the city and the secular spaces of the complex, such as the entrance hall and auditorium, which can be reached from street level. There is a powerful distinction between secular and sacred, as in traditional mosque design. True to the spirit of pioneering Islamic architects, Hadid used the most advanced mathematical concepts available at the time to generate form that responds to function.

Esra Akcan is currently a PhD candidate at the Graduate School of Architecture, Columbia University, New York. She also teaches graduate seminars at Columbia University and Parsons School of Design. She has received fellowships and scholarships from Columbia University, KRESS/ARIT, DAAD, the Mellon Foundation, Kinne and Graham Foundation, and has both taught and practised in Turkey. Her articles have been published widely, and her book, *Land(Fill) Istanbul: Twelve Scenarios for a Global City*, was published earlier in 2004.

Mohammad al-Asad is an architect and architectural historian, and the founding director of the Center for the Study of the Built Environment (CSBE), Amman, Jordan. He has a PhD in the history of architecture and has held post-doctorate positions at Harvard and the Institute for Advanced Study, Princeton. He has taught at the University of Jordan, Princeton University, MIT and the University of Illinois. He is author of numerous publications on the architecture of the Islamic world.

Turgut Cansever is an architect and urban planner. He has a PhD in art history, and has developed a conceptual approach based on a search for regional expression in architecture. He established his own architectural practice in 1951. Among his best-known projects are the Anatolian Club Hotel (1951–6) and the Demir Holiday Village in Bodrum, Turkey (1971). As a planner, he has headed projects in Istanbul on restoration and preservation, pedestrian zoning and metropolitan development. He is the winner of three Aga Khan Awards, and was appointed to the panel of the Master Jury of the Aga Khan Awards for Architecture in 1983.

Keith Critchlow is director of the educational charity Kairos and founder of VITA, and currently professor emeritus of the Visual Islamic and Traditional Arts department of the Prince of Wales Institute of Architecture, London. He was a consultant for the King Abdul Aziz University in Jeddah by Arthur Erickson Architects, and worked with Hassan Fathy on overall principles and design pattern language for the entire campus. He is the author of many books, and cofounder and architectural advisor to *Temenos* magazine on the arts of the imagination.

Mohamed El-Husseiny is an architect who was educated and trained in Egypt and the US. He worked with local and international firms within Egypt and the UK before starting his own practice in Cairo in 1987. His interest is mainly on reusing and developing viable elements of traditional and vernacular architecture in a modern and progressive context.

Sabiha Foster is a poet, architect and designer. She is a former director and design director of Foster and Partners. She has an MPhil in Islamic art and architecture, and has worked on the concept and design for many international projects, notably the Reichstag in Berlin. Her interests include comparative religion, psychology and current affairs. She is associated with the International League for Human Rights on post-conflict community-regeneration projects, and also works as an architecture and design consultant.

Jeremy Melvin is a contributing editor to *Architectural Design*, author of *FRS Yorke and the Evolution of English Modernism* (2003), and consultant to the Royal Academy's architecture programme. He writes and speaks about architecture extensively. He studied architecture and history of architecture at the Bartlett, UCL.

Majd Musa is an architect at the Center for the Study of the Built Environment (CSBE) in Amman, Jordan. She holds a masters degree in architecture, and has practised in the UAE and Jordan. She has co-authored a number of essays on architecture, urban planning and landscape architecture.

Suha Özkan is an architect, historian and theorist. He has been secretary-general of the Aga Khan Award for Architecture in Geneva since 1991. In 2002 he was elected as a council member (Region II) of the International Union of Architects (UIA), and will be president of the UIA's XXII Congress in Istanbul in 2005. He has undertaken extensive research on the theory and history of architecture, design, vernacular form and emergency housing, and published numerous articles and monographs. He is co-chair of the Sustainable Architecture task force of the Hassan Fathy Institute and the United Nations Centre for Human Settlements (Habitat) in support of the Habitat Agenda.

William R Polk is the senior director of the WP Carey Foundation. He taught for several years at Harvard University. During the Kennedy and Johnson administrations he was a member of the Policy Planning Council of the US Department of State, where he was in charge of planning US policy for most of the Islamic world. In 1965 he became professor of history at the University of Chicago and founded its Middle Eastern Studies Center. He later became president of the Adlai Stevenson Institute of International Affairs. His latest book, *Understanding Iraq*, will be published in January 2005.

Nasser Rabbat is the Aga Khan Professor of Islamic Architecture at MIT, where he has taught since 1991. His scholarly interests include the history and historiography of Islamic art, architecture and urbanism, and postcolonial criticism. His books include: *The Citadel of Cairo: A New Interpretation of Royal Mamluk Architecture* (1995) and *Thaqafat al Bina' wa Bina' al-Thaqafa* (The Culture of Building and Building Culture) (2002). His 2003 lectures at the Institut du Monde Arabe will be published under the title *L'art islamique à la recherche d'une méthode historique*.

David B Roosevelt is a senior advisor to the United Nations World Food Programme. His professional career spans more than 35 years in senior management positions in philanthropy and the investment and financial services sectors. His philanthropic activities include numerous board positions with a variety of both national and international foundations and NGOs. He is the author of a critically acclaimed biography, *Grandmerè: A Personal History of Eleanor Roosevelt* (2002).

Fariborz Sahba trained in Iran, where he has been head of design teams for various architectural firms. He has been involved in the design of a wide range of buildings, including Tehran's Centre of Handicraft Production and Arts Workshops, and the Iranian Embassy in Beijing, China. He was recognised in 1974 by Iran's Ministry of Housing for his design of a low-cost housing system. He is the designer of the Baha'i House of Worship (1986), also known as the Lotus Temple, in New Delhi. The temple is one of the most complicated and challenging structures of the 20th century.

Hashim Sarkis is the Aga Khan professor for landscape architecture and urbanism in Muslim societies at the Harvard University Graduate School of Design. He is also a practising architect between Cambridge, Massachusetts, and his hometown Beirut. His projects range from housing to institutional, urban and landscape design, and include a housing project for the fishermen of Tyre, a community centre in Mejdlaya, North Lebanon, and a small park in downtown Beirut. He is author of several publications.

Barbara Smith has spent most of her life as a writer and foreign editor for *The Economist*, during which time she was its Washington Bureau chief for six years. She retired very recently from her post as international editor for the Middle East and Africa. She has known many of the major political figures and leaders involved in Middle Eastern politics. For the last 30 years, her writing for *The Economist* has played a significant part in raising international awareness of Middle Eastern issues.

Doğan Tekeli is an architect and engineer. In 1954 he founded the Site architectural firm with Sami Sisa, which is the oldest architectural practice in modern Turkey. Between 1961 and 1971 he taught architectural design classes at the Istanbul Technical University (ITU) architectural department. He has also been a jury member and steering committee member for the Aga Khan architectural programme. In 2000 he was granted an honorary doctorate by the ITU Senate for his outstanding and life-long commitment to the profession of architecture.

SINAN HASSAN:

Finding New Words for Old Meanings

An architect of our times, Sinan Hassan has a strong affinity with his native Syria, as well as a pronounced awareness of international architectural trends and thinking. **Sabiha Foster** describes how Sinan, who spent a decade studying in the us, has been able to nurture his practice in Damascus and pursue his love of geometry, which is inspired as much by his own cultural and personal background as his education at SCI-ARC.

Sinan Hassan is an artist, poet and architect. Poetry is part of the fabric of Islamic culture, but to understand quite how difficult it has been for a contemporary Syrian to create a place for himself as an architect of his time, one has to look at the Syrian condition.

I have a numinous memory of the early 8th-century Umayyad Mosque[1] in Damascus. Its aisles of double-height horseshoe arches and a 13th-century minaret dedicated to Christ[2] symbolise the potency of Syria's rich heritage. The mosque, a masterpiece of architectural ingenuity, incorporates the three key elements of 'Islamic' architecture: the horseshoe arch[3], the *maqsurah*[4] and the square minaret. It is associated with Salah al-din al-Ayyubi, 'Saladin', who fought the Crusaders, belonged to a Sufi order and initiated the singing in this mosque of *nawbat*, hymns designed to inspire the listener into *sama*, a state of spiritual hearing.

Until the 20th century, Syria was a vast region incorporating the areas we now call Syria, Lebanon, Palestine, Israel and Jordan. It is heir to the civilisations of the ancient Egyptians, Babylonians, Hittites, Chaldeans and Persians. It has been part of Alexander the Great's empire, a Roman and, then, a Byzantine province. Conquered by the Muslims in AD 636, Syria became part of various Islamic empires. The Crusaders took a corner of the Umayyad Empire at the end of the 11th century and were overthrown by Salah-al-din al-Ayyubi at the end of the 12th century.

Later, Syria became part of the Turkish Ottoman Empire. By the beginning of the First World War, as the Ottoman Empire was crumbling, the 'Arabs' agreed to cooperate with the Allies in return for a British guarantee of independence for all Islamic lands under Ottoman rule. Britain and France reneged on the guarantee, and the same year secretly signed the Sykes-Picot agreement, by which they created the state of Israel and gave themselves most of the Arab lands under former Ottoman Turkish rule. Resistance to French administration began in Syria in 1944; its objective was to re-establish a 'Syrian-Arab' state that would include its original areas of present-day Lebanon, Syria, Jordan, Palestine and Israel. But the attempt failed and, in 1946, the Syrian-Arab Republic had to settle for its present-day boundaries and, finding itself betrayed and isolated, an anti-Western and pro-Soviet policy.

Resentment towards the West intensified when France and Britain attacked Egypt in 1956. After October 1957, the former USSR began to provide Syria with aid for the construction of many large-scale development projects. In the 1967 Arab–Israeli War, Syria lost the Golan Heights to Israel and, in November 1970, General Hafiz al-Assad became president. Al-Assad died in 2000, after a 30-year rule, and has been replaced by his son, President Bashar al-Assad. Syria has proven reserves of oil and gas, and the new president has embarked on a series of promising reforms.

The 2 Circles Apartment
Each of the apartments represents an episode in a serial
experiment that takes the circle as a dominant design element.
The circle's concave side creates intimacy and privacy – that is,
interiorisation and introversion – while its convex side creates
a sense of outsideness, exteriorisation and extraversion. The
design is based on two juxtaposed and superimposed circles
inscribed within a classically symmetrical and orthogonal
enclosure. These two circles define the major functional zones
in the layout and create a potent demarcation between the
private and the public. Two perpendicular axes, which
represent the principal organisational spines, run through
the plan from one end to the other, creating a strong sense
of axiality along which sculpted spaces are sequentially and
hierarchically arranged. These spaces proceed from the
very public to the very private in dramatically fluid transition,
through the continuous interplay of concavity and convexity.
Materials convey the tactile aspect and create a sense of
interiorised exterior as well as exteriorised interior.

On an individual scale, Sinan represents an active and positive
part of this vital period of transition.

Sinan returned to Damascus in 1996 after studying in the
US with, and under, a group of contemporary architects, critics
and educators including Eric Moss at SCI-ARC and Charles
Jencks at UCLA. He found himself either in the midst of state-
controlled politically motivated public sectors blindly
supportive of 'heritage and identity', or in crassly commercial
private sectors. Sinan survived his studio's start-up period by
designing apartment interiors whilst entering multiple national
competitions. He soon discovered the 'conciliatory award
syndrome' as underqualified local juries often manipulated
the course of events and rejected his proposals in favour of
mediocre designs.

For a while, Sinan imagined that his future in
architecture might mean that he had to 'settle for
winning praises from the audience more than prizes
from juries'. But Syria was on the move, albeit at its
own pace. Sinan did eventually go on to win a series
of important national competitions that included the
design for a new parliament building (1986), a new
Foreign Ministry building (1999) and the design for
a City Hall civic centre for Damascus (2003). None
of these projects has yet been realised, but they are
significant victories. Construction of a Ministry of
Communications project began in the summer, and the
first phase of the construction of the City Hall civic
centre is also scheduled to begin before the end of 2004.

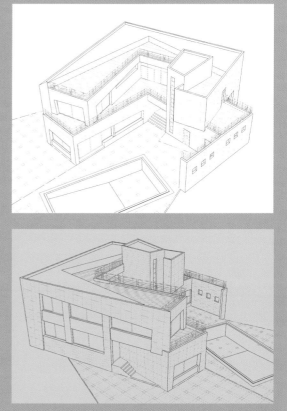

The 2 Us House

The house is composed of two interlocked U-shaped parts, a version of Deconstructivist architecture, a contemporary take on a traditional theme dressed and rendered in local materials and colours. Thematically, the house takes on the idea of differentiated vertical and horizontal stacking in the form of concentric rectangular framing; that is, frames within frames. Based on the square form, the theme of abstract and flat geometric ornamental patterns is made volumetric and given architectural meaning and presence.

Mathematically, the overall radial and rotational composition combines different geometric ordering systems. A rectilinear system, represented in the house itself as a double-U configuration, is manipulated but mathematically controlled. A curvilinear system is represented in the surrounding buildings and landscape. The presence of the circle, although subliminal, can be discerned at three different levels of manifestation: firstly in the concentric circular shape of the entry court and the encircling buildings; secondly in the radial arrangement of the landscape and ground terraces; and thirdly in the underlying organisational principle governing the rotational pattern of the two U-shaped components and their radial alignment.

The two U-shaped parts merge vertically, as they overlap and collide, in two spaces: at the double-height living room and at the stairway, which acts as the rotational anchor. Other points of convergence are the hinging circular column in the open breakfast area that acts as a transition between inside and outside, and the sharp edge at the very corner of the house where the tension between the two grids reaches its peak, culminating in a blade-like joint.

Terraces pinwheel so as to circumvent the central courtyard and to offer maximum view and afford minimum exposure. They remain protected, as privacy is the main concern and preoccupation in a predominantly conservative society. Portals and fenestration elements are treated as spatial, rather than flat, elements, whereby each window is composed of two different layers – a window within a window: an internal window responding to practical and pragmatic requirements, and an external one responding to formal and conceptual conditions.

Similarly, the entrance is emphasised through a multiframed vertical portal – a door within a door. When the main door is closed, the house appears to be conventionally thick and forbidding. But when the door is opened, it appears to be nothing more than a thin urban threshold between an entry court at the front and a courtyard at the back, and represents no more than a filter between an exteriorised interior and an interiorised exterior.

The house is clad in local white stone and black basalt.

Now that Syria has embarked on a new phase of reform and development, Sinan says that the construction industry is improving 'in terms of local and imported technologies, systems and building materials'. One understands, therefore, that it is not easy 'by any means and all measures, to execute high-quality designs in such an environment'.

Until recently, designing for government has been exclusively restricted to governmental consultation agencies or, bizarrely, to faculty members of the state university. Commissioning for public works was therefore previously impossible. But it seems that now, under certain criteria, it is becoming possible for large firms to get public commissions if they accept 'third priority' status. The other good news is that national design competitions are gaining momentum – to the point of becoming trendy, but at least this makes it possible for small unconventional practices (like Sinan's studio of himself plus a few assistants) or even independent individuals to get public works. Of course, this can only happen if the competition is well administered, which is the excruciating exception and not the general rule. Nevertheless, this is exactly how Sinan obtained the City Hall civic centre project and the Communications Ministry commission, for both of which he went into joint ventures with large firms of building contractors.

This laborious process is an indication of Sinan's struggles. He says he 'relies on luck and divine intervention as well as on personal connections, hard work and an understanding of what one's up against'. He is convinced that Syria is on the road to a sensible process of democratisation and, although he has no local support, he remains firmly committed to a reformist public policy in local architecture. With the grit and determination he has already shown, there seems little doubt that Sinan will do more than succeed.

In the last decades, as a result of rapidly increasing populations, cities like Damascus and Aleppo, which had maintained their ancient and rich traditions of craftsmanship, have been in the throes of building booms that led developers and the construction industry to focus on fast profits with utter disregard for notions of quality and craftsmanship. Highly talented craftspeople are now few and far between, and Sinan relies on a workforce of individual artisanship, along with local versions of modern production and construction technology. He also has access to a few imported systems, mainly in the area of glazing (curtain walls and tempered glass), aluminium panels, cladding and dry fixing systems, along with spider steel structural systems and primitive computerised woodwork, all of which have just recently been introduced to the local building market. These systems have immense potential, but workforces are poorly paid and poorly educated. All this impinges on efficiency and productivity.

Architecturally, such conditions must have an impact on the level of formal complexity to begin with, and on the quality of the outcome. As Sinan admits: 'It takes its toll on the nerve system of any near-perfectionist designer.' But he does soldier on, and seems to manage well; with a great deal of supervision and successful collaboration with friends in the construction business, he says he can 'maintain very high standards, relatively speaking', that combine the virtues of the local and imported materials and technologies, and of skilled local, individually based workmanship.

Sinan refers to architects in the Middle East who have been inspired by the spirit of the place, and these include Hassan Fathy, Abdul Wahed El-Wakil, Abdul Halim, Rifat Chadirji, Mohammed Makyya and Basel Al-Bayyati, and later Rasem Badran and Jaafar Tukan from Jordan. There are others like Hani Rasheed and Zaha Hadid who have studied in the West but seem dissociated from the history and the culture of the places they came from. Sinan pins his colours to the mast. He is, he says, 'a local, but not locally confined, progressive but not trendy, rooted and yet forward looking'.

Sinan does not believe in collective authorship and does not suffer from any illusions or pretensions regarding this issue: 'I give priority to individual over collective or generic identity. Of course, I do also believe

in collaboration and cooperation, and in controlled and well-orchestrated and directed teamwork.' Sinan's studio consists of himself and 'only two or three very good young assistants'.

In the past, Islamic artists and architects were masters of geometry. Sinan's interest in geometry has to do with his early affinity with Euclidian geometry and his familiarity with abstract geometric Islamic art. Geometry, he says, 'is an interface and common language, in terms of vocabulary and syntax, between art and architecture in our part of the world'. He says he is indebted to his US education, at SCI-ARC in particular and under Eric Moss, whose geometry and method of design, along with that of Eisenman of the 1980s 'had its conscious and subconscious influence on me, perhaps more so, I feel, than on, say, Hadid or Libeskind'. Yet Sinan feels that, essentially, his passion for geometry stems from his own personal nature and

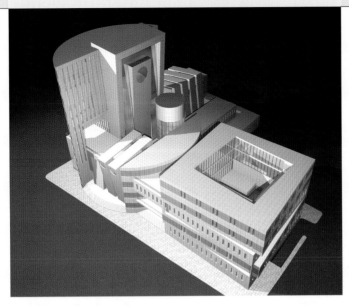

cultural background, which allowed him to synthesise geometry and poetry in his work: 'The ornamental stems directly from my general cultural roots and Islamic art, the sentimental from my personal encounter with the realm of poetry, and the mental from my early affinity with Euclidian geometry but developed greatly in the US.' Of course, these influences relate to aesthetics, thematics and semantics, the last relating to his interest in mathematics and geometry. Sinan says this abstract facet 'matured, perceptually and conceptually, and developed to become less platonic and more tectonic, less extrusive and more intrusive, less plane and more spatial, less simplistic or structuralist and more complex, and "Deconstructivist" if you will'.

Sinan is the consequence of two opposing ideologies and methodologies, which challenge him to reconcile conventional, rational Damascus with unconventional and irrational Los Angeles. The opposing tensions are apparent in his designs and raise questions he is all too conscious of. Can a work of architecture be at the same time local and global? Can we transcend the traditional and contemporary, the eternal and temporary, the elemental and complex, the rational and

irrational, the intellectual and experiential? Can we reconcile the particular and general, and the familiar and different? Can this confrontation be resolved? Can we possibly find new meanings for old words, and new words for old meanings?

These are the very questions architecture itself needs to face if it is to evolve beyond its present tendency to veer towards being just another glossy commodity. Can we, architecturally, speak a universal and contemporary language in a local tongue? Can we talk about identity and local heritage in terms other than the formalistic and stylistic? And how can a work of architecture speak simultaneously of its place and time?

Architecture is life. Therefore, feeling and thinking – the two opposite functions in human psychology – must inevitably affect Sinan's creative expression, his being-in-the-world. Generally speaking, people tend to be led by their dominant function only to be tripped up sooner or later by their repressed function. Sinan the artist and poet seems to have embraced his latent rational potential. His designs show a conscious attempt at alchemical resolution via irrationally rational expression.

As one who finds no contradiction between place and space, and who can belong to Syria and be of the world, Sinan Hassan is an architect for our times. Δ+

Sinan Hassan Resumé

1985	Received BArch from Damascus University (ranking first in the year)
1986	Won a national competition in Syria for a new parliament building
1990	Gained MArch from SCI-ARC
1994	Received MArch (urban architecture) from USC.
1996	MA in architecture (HTC) from UCLA
1996	Upon his permanent return to Damascus, resumed private professional practice, winning several local and national design competitions
1999	Won a national competition for new Foreign Ministry building in Syria
2002	Translated and edited (with introduction) the Arabic version of Ismail Sirajeldin book *Architecture and Society*, published by the Library of Alexandria
2003	Won competition for the design of a City Hall civic centre for Damascus
2003	Published and authored two books of Arabic poetry.

Notes
1 In AD 705, the caliph Walid, a patron of architecture, bought the derelict site from local Christians and began construction. The relics of St John the Baptist, revered in the Koran as the Prophet Yahya, were incorporated in a shrine within the mosque. L Golvyn, 'Essai sur l'architecture religieuse musulmane',Tome 2, *L'Art Religieux des Umayyades de Syrie*, Klinocksiek, 1971; *Guide des Lieux de Pelerinages* by al Harawi, Abu al Hassan, Abu Bakr (died AD 1215). Translation 1957, referred to by L Golvyn.
2 Revered in the Koran as the Prophet Issa.
3 Used structurally and decoratively in this instance.
4 A screen of timber or brick, which gave the caliph and his attendants reserved seats for prayer.

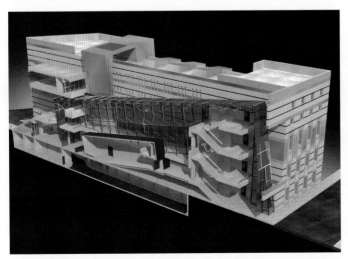

Temporary
Housing for
Workers in Iraq

In post-conflict situations, housing becomes a matter of pragmatic
provision. **Bruce Stewart** looks at how an Oman-based contractor sought
a prefabricated solution to accommodating its employees on site in Iraq.

In a volatile situation, fraught with dangers, the rebuilding and
rebalancing of Iraq is now under way. To help the country's
move towards democratic stability, several non-Iraqi
contractors are involved in the process of getting the systems
in place to support the transfer of power. One of these
companies, Oman-based Renaissance Services SAOG, has been
in Iraq for some time now, providing services back-up for the
various groups of personnel currently based there. These
service contracts were won in the face of strong multinational
competition, and now ensure that one of Iraq's near
neighbours is involved at a practical level.

The initial setup of the company in Iraq was a logistical
nightmare as the contract required that it had to be on site and
fully functional within a very short time frame. This time
pressure, combined with the scale of the operation, made the
choice of accommodation required for the company's
employees simple. To house the 700 new workers quickly, with
good minimum standards of comfort and domestic services,
in view of the of the often inhospitable nature of the landscape,
extreme heat, and with almost no permanent impact on the
environment, meant that prefabricated units were the only
viable option. However, this solution is not new to the area;
much of the workers' accommodation in the oilfield areas of
the whole Middle Eastern region consists of prefabricated
encampments of various types.

The housing units were chosen from a standard range

available at short notice from a supplier in Dubai, and
are of a very simple, relatively lightweight design. The
need for quick, low-tech construction methods meant
that completely finished units were selected, the basic
units being not unlike simplified versions of American
trailer homes. The materials and building methods
are also simple. A base 'skid' of a grid of 140
millimetres by 73 millimetres by 10.5 kilograms/metre
MS (mild steel) I beams supports the whole structure.
Timber joists then support 18-millimetre plywood
decking, to which the appropriate floor finish is applied:
2-millimetre vinyl tiles in domestic spaces. Walls are
lightweight, consisting of heavy external paint on 4-
millimetre plywood, and an internal finish of 3-
millimetre board sandwiching 42-millimetre expanded
polystyrene insulation supported by studwork at
610-millimetre centres. The ceiling is paint-finished
plywood on a timber frame, with 0.45-millimetre
lightweight metal profile sheet finish for the roof
carried by timber purlins on 25 millimetre x 25
millimetre MS angle roof trusses. This shell can
then be adapted to various functional permutations.

Managerial staff are housed in two-roomed units
with built-in sanitary provisions, and manual workers
are in small dormitory modules serviced by shower
blocks. Initial setup is straightforward: the site is

Below
While the prefabricated buildings are quite basic, the finishes and decoration of the interior can create comfortable spaces. Once again, the flexibility of the system is crucial – communal showers and toilets are provided using another variation of the system.

cleared and levelled and the units brought in by lorry. They are then lowered into place by a 20-ton crane, on to very simple foundations consisting of concrete blocks at each corner and two intermittent positions. Utilities are a simple 'hook- up' system that allows for water, drainage and electrical connections. Electrical power is provided from a generated supply. As the temperature in this region can easily exceed 30°C, all the units have access points and support brackets for air-conditioning units.

Due to the nature of the area in which the development is situated, the employees are very much restricted to the site when not working. It is therefore important that a variety of facilities are provided beyond provisions for sleeping and washing. Kitchens and dining rooms, laundry rooms, recreation and TV rooms and mosque structures are all provided using variations of the basic prefabricated module. The personalisation of the space by the employees happens quickly. Apart from the usual putting up of pictures of home and family (all the workers are non-Iraqi, coming predominantly from India, Sri Lanka and the Philippines), they have appropriated the space outside their units to create paved garden areas with shading, which are suitable for barbeques and various sporting activities. Maintenance for the site is simple and carried out by a team of workers who are given basic training, tools, manuals and spare parts, and thus most faults can be repaired swiftly and easily.

Using an easily transported system allows large groups of people to be housed efficiently and comfortably. 'Design' is not a major criterion of these prefabricated buildings: functional requirements such as siting and the ready provision of shelter are the primary objectives. It is the stamp of the individual both internally and externally that breathes life into these structures. This is very much in keeping with Henri Lefebvre's notions of lived space – space that has meaning only once it is inhabited. Interestingly, Lefebvre's thoughts on ephemeral space can also be seen to apply to these spatial arrangements:

Although work ... demands a fixed location this is not true of sleep or play and in this respect the West might do well to learn from the East with its great open spaces and low easily moved furniture.[1]

Currently, all the employees are male, living away from home, so there is no call for the wider range of facilities that, in what is basically a small village, would usually be required to support families and family needs. However, the transformable nature of the structures means they could, if necessary, be adapted for many other uses, such as school rooms, libraries, offices and family homes.

Although the contracts won by Renaissance Services are by their nature short term, the accommodation units are robust enough to have a life exceeding five years. The site can, and will, be dismantled as quickly as it was erected, enabling the area to return to its original state without a lasting impact on the local environment.

Perhaps the single most important issue concerning these prefabricated buildings is what will become of them at the completion of the company's contracts in Iraq. It would be very easy to imagine that a very competitive commercial operation would relocate the units to its next project site in order to maximise initial expenditure, however this is not the case here. The site will be taken down and the units moved, but they will stay in Iraq to be used as temporary housing, schools and shops for the Iraqi people. This mobility is in a way very appropriate, echoing as it does the nomadic, Bedouin history of Arabic peoples. As mentioned, it is the very simplicity of these structures that is the key to their success. Δ+

Temporary Housing Iraq	G 0-29%	F 30-39%	E 40%	D 41-49%	C 50-59%	B 60-69%	A 70-100%
QUALITATIVE							
Space-Interior				D			
Space-Exterior				D			
Location			E				
Community					C		
QUANTITATIVE							
Construction Cost						B	
Cost-rental/purchase	Not Applicable						
Cost in use					C		
Sustainability							A
AESTHETICS							
Good Design?				D			
Appeal				D			
Innovative?					C		

This table is based on an analytical method of success in contributing to solution to housing need. The criteria are: Quality of life – does the project maintain or improve good basic standards? Quantative factors – has the budget achieved the best it can? Aesthetics – does the building work visually?

Notes
1 Henri Lefebvre, 'The production of space', in Neil Leach, *Re-thinking Architecture*, Routledge (London), 1997, p 145.

Bruce Stewart, with Jane Briginshaw, is currently researching and writing *The Architects' Navigation Guide to New Housing*, to be published in autumn 2005 by Wiley-Academy. Bruce Stewart trained as an architect and is currently a course teacher at the Bartlett School of Architecture, UCL London.

Background
'Command' wallpaper (shown in blue) takes inspiration from Internet chatrooms. This pattern, which debuted in spring 2004, explores the symbolic visual language of electronic communication. Perhaps it's no surprise to discover 'Commmand' and several other Knoll wall coverings are by the graphics firm 2x4. (The company has led branding exercises for both Knoll and wall-covering producer Wolf-Gordon; Knoll press materials praise the 'fresh, intellectual result'.) Viewed from afar, 'Command' reads as a mossy texture cut-through with vertical rivers of negative space. But up close, the humour is hard to miss. Myriad exclamation points punctuate the neat rows of characters. 'You can't possibly be that enthusiastic,' says 2x4 partner Georgianna Stout.

Architectural
Graphics Standards

Craig Kellogg mounts the case for putting graphic designers into the architecture game.

Westerners will discount traditional Islamic art and architecture for its intricate patterning. Is decoration a design no-no, or a question of fashion? Heavy 'Oriental' patterns were nurtured and encouraged by 19th-century Orientalists. And every style of applied decoration captured imaginations in the 1970s. Perhaps it's time again to take inspiration from the intuitive flourish of Islamic calligraphy, Chinese carpets or glazed tiles from Andalucia?

It was a full-scale backlash against the Postmodernism of the mid-1990s that saw even Robert Venturi and Denise Scott Brown give up their decorated sheds sheathed in big blousy floral patterns or American flags. But haven't we now shifted sufficiently so that those architects reaching for added zing can start to look beyond the restrained application of solid colour for walls?

Creating patterned surfaces demands a knack for thinking in two dimensions. (Architects are nothing if not three-dimensional thinkers.) Since two-dimensional acrobatics are a snap for trained graphic designers, companies like graphics agency 2x4 are entering the architectural arena. For a start, 2x4 designed a pivotal special issue of the periodical *Architecture New York* (better known as *ANY*) guest-edited by Rem Koolhaas. Subsequently, alongside branding work for Wolf-Gordon and Knoll, 2x4 has presented architectural exhibitions. But it is the potted history of its collaborations with Koolhaas that provides a snapshot of this company's increasing influence in the architectural world.

Once *ANY* had matched 2x4 with Koolhaas a decade ago – though separated by an ocean and a generation – they never lost touch. Today their collaborations have 'a kind of blurring of authorship,' says Georgianna Stout, one of three partners at 2x4. Koolhaas' troubled Guggenheim Las Vegas was an early outing in three dimensions for the group. The signage conceived by 2x4 was etched directly into Koolhaas' rusty facade.

The firm's efforts for Prada – another Koolhaas client – began as a website development project. Before long, Koolhaas had engaged 2x4 for multiple features within his New York 'epicentre' for Prada, in SoHo. Among the highlights were digital videos and a riotous (gargantuan) digital wallpaper mural. The store had been open only nine months before an impressionistic Asian crowd scene from 2x4 replaced the original floral pattern the firm had composed of pixelated bits from naughty videos. Currently on the wall, floor-to-ceiling nude humanoids – plasticised, bald, genitalia discreet – romp through a photorealistically rendered, vaguely alpine Eden.

Prada recently debuted another 'epicentre', this time in LA. But it is the Illinois Institute of Technology (IIT) that supplies textbook examples of 2x4's signature blunt surface message, concealing a more complex idea underneath. 'It becomes an intellectual activity,' 2x4 partner Michael Rock admits. What appears to be a portrait of Ludwig Mies van der Rohe fritted

on to the glass surrounding the entrance is revealed, upon closer inspection, to be a composite image assembled from stick figures – each one engaged in an activity such as eating, sleeping, studying. As Rock notes, students enter and exit the building through Mies's mouth.

The supergraphic imagery at IIT grew out of an idea to cloak the interiors with advertising at billboard scale. The concept, Rock explains, was to rent the walls, giving the advertisers the responsibility for keeping the murals updated. When the school quashed the concept, calling it too commercial, 2x4 covered some of the walls with superflocked paper from a factory set up for manufacturing wood-grain paint rollers. Simpler still, unpainted gypsum board – a finish detail at Prada New York that has also popped up in several other Koolhaas projects – has been silk-screened with arabesque traceries.

The firm seems capable of anything, but Rock was not trained specifically to work in three dimensions and says: 'You can't be experts in everything.' True, perhaps. Then again, the most surprising puzzle piece at IIT is a stunningly three-dimensional starburst chandelier assembled from fluorescent tubes. As Rock's clients eagerly hopscotch through an ever wider range of experiments with him – from Web design to branding, to signage, to wrapping-paper patterns and chandeliers – the firm is widening its scope. For Rock and Stout, who seem almost unnaturally sweet-tempered, it is part of the business strategy. They have proven themselves steady and fearless, a valuable resource for their architectural collaborators. And, as Rock says, each new client, no matter how small, has the potential to become repeat business 'for as long as they'll have us'. ∆+

Herzog & de Meuron, Schaulager Laurenz Foundation, Münchenstein, Basel, Switzerland, 2000–03
Below
Between the small entrance pavilion and the large volume, a tense dynamism opens up, mixing the physical and the mnemonic.

Schaulager
Laurenz
Foundation

In the Basel suburbs, Herzog & de Meuron has created a *schaulager*, or 'show storage', for an unusual private foundation. Jeremy Melvin explains how, in this great warehouse for storing art, the architects have not only worked with a scale that ranges from the domestic to the industrial, but also sought to underline 'architecture's physicality' while manipulating the ephemeral play of light within the building.

Creating 'new means of expression that look into the future'
is very likely to produce work that is 'not yet generally
understood in the present'. This underlying discrepancy
between the visionary and current perceptions was outlined
by the Deed of the Emanuel Hoffmann Foundation. The
foundation had been set up in 1933 with the express intention
of bridging this gap. Established by Maja Hoffmann-Stehlin
(later Stehlin-Sacher, a name change that has less to do
with torte than contemporary music), it was founded to
commemorate her first husband who had died in a car crash.
The work continues, and its recent initiatives include the
endowment of a chair at Basel University through the Laurenz
Foundation in memory of a great-grandson of Frau Hoffmann
who died prematurely, and creating an institution to promote
the different means of interpreting, studying, preserving,
storing and displaying its new and unfamiliar forms of art.

This is the Schaulager – literally meaning show storage
– a powerful, roughcast-concrete form in the Basel suburb
of Münchenstein, designed by Herzog & de Meuron. It might
seem to epitomise those roots in the tangible and physical
that seem to make architecture an unlikely bedfellow for
contemporary art, as it has increasingly veered towards the
ephemeral, transitory and illusory. Buildings provide the
necessary storage space, modulation of environmental
conditions and control points for visitors, chained to the
tangible and shackled to function, but architecture would seem
to have little place in art's new lines of enquiry. It might all
be as Hegel explained. Though architecture played a vital role
in the great project of *Der Aesthetik* by giving a tangible shape
to the 'spirit' that motivated social rituals, it quickly became
obsolete once artists realised that spirit might actually
enter, rather than wrap around, the outside of form. As art
progressed through sculpture, painting music and poetry,
architecture became increasingly redundant, as 'spirit' found
ever more sophisticated means of expression.

Herzog & de Meuron's design is a powerful counterblast
to such assumptions. It recognises, and even stresses,
architecture's physicality, consciously contrasting the
roughcast texture with a smooth, white finish on the entrance
facade. But it also finds an aspect of that physicality which,
perhaps paradoxically, takes architecture close to the condition
of contemporary conceptual art. Architecture, though physical,
lacks the potential for literal expression of painting, sculpture
or literature. Like conceptual art it communicates by evoking
illusions, ideas, associations and impressions it can neither
contain nor make immanent. As volumes fill out, textures
change, or different light sources reveal new sights, spaces
open for the imagination to fill. No architects understand this
better than Herzog & de Meuron, and nowhere has the firm
exploited these effects better than in the entrance at the
Schaulager Laurenz Foundation.

In Basel, everyone travels by tram, and the provision of
special stops for the Schaulager and Renzo Piano's Beyeler
Foundation suggests that taxpayers get something from the

public subsidies they fund. It also means that the
experience of reaching the Schaulager is shared in
contrast, say, to London's Royal Opera House where
it varies between arrival by a chauffeur-driven car
and progression to a box, or a walk on foot from the
tube station to the upper tier of the amphitheatre.
Schaulager's location, explains Herzog & de Meuron
partner Harry Gugger, is 'programmatic'; it is at the
point where bonded warehouses give way to suburban
houses. This itself proclaims the Schaulager's
difference from a city-centre museum and similarity
to a town fringe store, but it also sets a condition that
the design elaborates.

The small 'entrance house' belongs to the scale of
suburbia, while the concrete box relates to, and is, at
least in part, a warehouse. These conditions are simply
stated, but the juxtaposition between them generates
a powerful dynamic. The precinct between both forms
takes on the role of an urban space, something between
home and public institution. Between the small,
solid volume and the concave, white-faced wall of the

Top
General view of the Schaulager Laurenz Foundation, a large cuboid volume that
combines the roughness of a warehouse and sophistication of an urban institution.

Bottom left
Basement-level plan.

Bottom right
Ground-level plan.

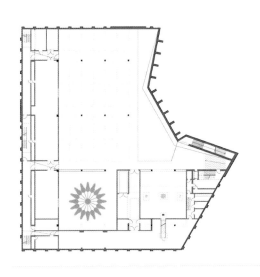

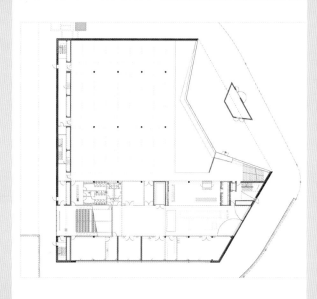

Top
Second-floor plan showing potential of division into small chambers.

Middle
Section through auditorium, loading bay, basement and storage cells.

Bottom
Section through exhibition space and storage cells..

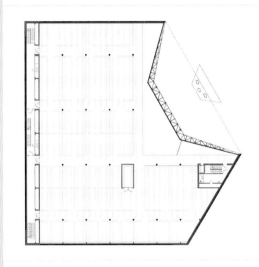

warehouse there is almost a physical tension, as if the larger building draws visitors out of its pint-sized neighbour. From here, too, there are views into the basement-level gallery where, once a year, there is an exhibition, and this combination of physical and visual connection might have continued had an original idea of using the pavilion as a projector room for throwing images on to the white walls materialised. As it is, those images appear on digital screens mounted on the walls.

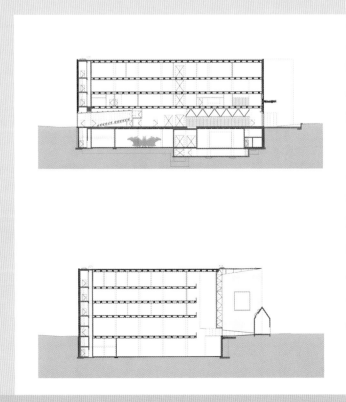

These physical distortions continue on the inside. It opens into a large, high volume with galleries marking the floors where artworks are stored, each item or connected group of items in its own cell where it can be studied, stored or conserved. But only scholars have access to them, and only by arrangement: the masses are prevented from entering these sancta because they do not have access cards, which are programmed to allow entry to rooms with only those works relevant to a particular course of study. During the annual exhibitions, held from May to September, visitors can descend via a ramp that entices, compresses and then liberates them into the gallery space. The foundation's first show, in 2003, was Dieter Roth; this year, Herzog & de Meuron themselves took over the gallery; next year it's Jeff Wall's turn.

In keeping with its self-declared status as a new type of art institution, processes like delivery and preparation for travel are made manifest. There are conservation studios, a lecture room and a café, which sits between a balcony overlooking the gallery and the loading bay. Some of the processes, as well as the product, of art become a spectacle. Throughout, the architecture strikes a balance between the naive and the knowing. At a quick glance the loading bay might be taken for the car deck on an Isle of Wight ferry, but that transportation system is not known for its carriage of contemporary art. The overarching idea, says Gugger, was to create a volume that allowed easy subdivision and redivision, an aim simply and frequently stated but rarely achieved. To this end he had originally envisaged an adobe construction to ensure an absolutely even climate with minimal mechanical servicing, but the time implications were insurmountable. Even with a more conventional concrete structure, the temperature maintains a constant 21°C, with 'a boiler the same size as the one in my house'.

All this might seem prosaic alongside, and without an intellectual connection to, the collection of art that was once too advanced to be understood. That collection is extraordinary. In the 1930s it was Arp, Dali and Klee; in the 1960s it went conceptual with Beuys, and has progressed to Nauman, Sherman, Kabakov and Wall. As Gugger explains, the foundation can no longer buy works of 'the Classic Modern period'; they are too familiar. But even more extraordinary are the ways in which Herzog & de Meuron has been able to infiltrate the ideas raised by that body of work with architecture; how the quotidian issues like arrival at a building, storage or climate control become physical and, therefore, commonly experienced starting points for speculation. Idiosyncratic it may be, but those idiosyncracies transform into ways of imagining the future. Δ+

Thunder Bay
Regional Health Sciences Centre

Sean Stanwick explains how a new hospital at Thunder Bay in northwestern Ontario seeks to challenge accepted truisms in health-care design.

That hospitals are designed with patient care and long-term functionality as key priorities is a basic expectation. Yet, as the maintenance of health care rises to the top of many municipal agendas, we must continually work to challenge these assumptions if we are to free ourselves from the grip of Sullivan's popular axiom of 'form follows function' and approach something closer to form, function and delight.

While there are guidelines that mandate the essentials of life safety, there are few that speak to the humanistic aspects of architecture. To this end, if the creation of architecture and the delivery of health care share the common goal of improving quality of life, then the role of health-care architecture has never been more relevant.

Positioning itself as a seminal project in this regard, the recently completed Thunder Bay Regional Health Sciences Centre embraces this responsibility and provides a dynamic and comforting healing environment. Knowing that a poorly designed facility will have a measurable negative impact on patient recovery, the project features a dramatic three-storey wood-and-glass walkway that curves to follow the path of the sun, to allow deep penetration of direct light and provide a panoramic vista of the verdant landscape. Conceived as a path through a forest, 'the corridor fosters a direct connection to nature,' says Tye Farrow, partner in charge of design at Farrow Partnership Architects, one of two successor firms to Salter Farrow Pilon Architects, the architects of the project.

With a population of approximately 120,000, Thunder Bay is located in northwestern Ontario, on the shores of Lake Superior. Born of a forced amalgamation of two adjacent communities, the city determined that it would be more economical to design one single regional facility, rather than renovating its two existing local hospitals. With a catchment area equal to the size of France, the project was largely completed in October 2003, with the first patients transferred in February 2004.

Of the site's 60 acres, only 35 are buildable, with the remainder consisting of a system of natural drainage channels and wetlands. Tying into this, the landscape strategy links a series of connected bogs and wetlands to cleanse and divert storm-water runoff, and also serve as a breeding area for indigenous cold-water fish species.

Conceptually, the building is planned in a T configuration, a main circulation spine serving as the organisational datum from which individual departments radiate, including a cancer centre, forensic mental health centre, maternity and child department, and 375 patient beds. At the junction of the T configuration is a planned space for an outdoor market, and a public amphitheatre, an amenity presently lacking in the community.

Architecturally, the project achieves a number of noteworthy design firsts. It is the first hospital in the country to use wood – a material with limited applications in the provincial building codes – as a primary structural element, and is also the first in Canada to bring direct sunlight into the cancer radiation bunkers without compromising user safety.

The most salient design aspect is the means through which the project references its cultural and physical context. Expressing the inherent poetics of shelter, comfort and healing, wood was used extensively within the structure of the main public area as it affords a warmer aesthetic and better reflects the history and economics of the region. Replete with a rugged vernacular of wood and stone, as is typical of the Canadian north, the region's history is owed largely to both the national railway that once helped unify the country, and to the pulp and paper industry, which is still a major employer in the area. In total, more than 1,100 pieces of glue-laminated members were used.

Beyond the project's material palette, the fundamental principle behind the design is a confidence in the value of humanism. 'As a paradigm for design,' says Farrow, 'humanism is rooted in the notion that patient wellbeing is of the utmost importance, and should manifest itself in visually pleasing environments that evoke images and sentiment through the use of natural materials, access to sunlight, and the marriage of architecture and landscape.'

In a region where daylight is limited, the benefits of direct sunlight must never be undervalued. In *The Biophilia Hypothesis* (1993), biologist EO Wilson wrote of our attachment to the natural environment, inferring that it is impossible to detach from nature without also compromising our spiritual existence. Supporting this is a 2003 study by the Commission for Architecture and the Built Environment (CABE) and the Royal College of Nursing (RCN), which concluded that 85 per cent of people surveyed agree that better-quality buildings improve the quality of people's lives, and ultimately reduce patient recovery times.

If Wilson, or Farrow, are indeed correct, why then would a community not embrace humanism? A common misconception is that it is financially difficult to reconcile functionality with qualitative designs. This is simply not true. When compared to steel, the cost of the wood structure was less, and clearly offers superior aesthetic value. Perhaps the measure of success lies in a hospital's ability to adapt to the varying needs of its community without compromising the underlying philosophy of humanism itself. As the qualitative results are self-evident, it is undeniably a challenge worth rising to. Δ+

Based in Toronto, Sean Stanwick is a regular contributor to Δ who has a particular interest in urban design and the themed spectacular. He has contributed to *Sustaining Architecture in the Anti-Machine Age*, and is currently writing *Interior Angles: Wine by Design* and *Interior Angles: Lofty Ideas* (all for Wiley). He is an instructor with the Royal Architectural Institute of Canada and is currently a design architect with Farrow Partnership Architects.

Subscribe Now

As an influential and prestigious architectural publication, *Architectural Design* has an almost unrivalled reputation worldwide. Published bimonthly, it successfully combines the currency and topicality of a newsstand journal with the editorial rigour and design qualities of a book. Consistently at the forefront of cultural thought and design since the 1960s, it has time and again proved provocative and inspirational – inspiring theoretical, creative and technological advances. Prominent in the 1980s for the part it played in Postmodernism and then in Deconstruction, ⚟ has recently taken a pioneering role in the technological revolution of the 1990s. With groundbreaking titles dealing with cyberspace and hypersurface architecture, it has pursued the conceptual and critical implications of high-end computer software and virtual realities. ⚟

⚟ Architectural Design

SUBSCRIPTION RATES 2004
Institutional Rate: UK £160
Personal Rate: UK £99
Discount Student* Rate: UK £70
OUTSIDE UK
Institutional Rate: US $240
Personal Rate: US $150
Student* Rate: US $105

*Proof of studentship will be required when placing an order. Prices reflect rates for a 2002 subscription and are subject to change without notice.

TO SUBSCRIBE
Phone your credit card order:
+44 (0)1243 843 828

Fax your credit card order to:
+44 (0)1243 770 432

Email your credit card order to:
cs-journals@wiley.co.uk

Post your credit card or cheque order to:
John Wiley & Sons Ltd.
Journals Administration Department
1 Oldlands Way
Bognor Regis
West Sussex PO22 9SA
UK

Please include your postal delivery address with your order.

All ⚟ volumes are available individually. To place an order please write to:
John Wiley & Sons Ltd
Customer Services
1 Oldlands Way
Bognor Regis
West Sussex PO22 9SA

Please quote the ISBN number of the issue(s) you are ordering.

⚟ is available to purchase on both a subscription basis and as individual volumes

○ I wish to subscribe to ⚟ *Architectural Design* at the **Institutional rate of £160**.

○ I wish to subscribe to ⚟ *Architectural Design* at the **Personal rate of £99**.

○ I wish to subscribe to ⚟ *Architectural Design* at the **Student rate of £70**.

○ ⚟ *Architectural Design* is available to individuals on either a calendar year or rolling annual basis; Institutional subscriptions are only available on a calendar year basis. Tick this box if you would like your Personal or Student subscription on a rolling annual basis.

○ Payment enclosed by Cheque/Money order/Drafts.

Value/Currency £/US$ _____

○ Please charge £/US$ _____
to my credit card.
Account number:

□□□□□□□□□□□□□□□□□

Expiry date:

□□□□□□

Card: Visa/Amex/Mastercard/Eurocard *(delete as applicable)*

Cardholder's signature _____

Cardholder's name _____

Address _____

_____

_____ Post/Zip Code _____

Recipient's name _____

Address _____

_____

_____ Post/Zip Code _____